the RIDDLE *of the* RAVEN

A Sailing Ship Possessed by a Ghost

JAN DE GROOT

Sono Nis Press
Winlaw, British Columbia

Library and Archives Canada Cataloguing in Publication
De Groot, Jan, 1932-
The riddle of the Raven : a sailing ship possessed
by a ghost / Jan de Groot.
ISBN 978-1-55039-183-1
1. Raven (Ketch). 2. Haunted places. 3. Sailing ships—Canada.
4. Ghosts—Canada. 5. De Groot, Jan, 1932-. I. Title.
BF1471.D44 2011   133.1′29   C2011-902368-7

Sono Nis Press most gratefully acknowledges support for our publishing program provided by the Government of Canada through the Canada Book Fund and the Canada Council for the Arts, and by the Province of British Columbia through the British Columbia Arts Council and the Book Publishing Tax Credit, Ministry of Provincial Revenue.

Edited by John Eerkes-Medrano
Copy edited by Audrey McClellan
Proofreading by Karla Decker
Cover and interior design by Jim Brennan
All photos, except for newspaper images, provided by
Steve and Sandy Mayes.

Published by
Sono Nis Press
Box 160
Winlaw, British Columbia
V0G 2J0
1-800-370-5228

books@sononis.com
www.sononis.com

Printed on acid-free paper that is forest friendly (100% post-consumer recycled paper) and has been processed chlorine free.

Printed and bound in Canada by Houghton Boston Printing.

CONTENTS

For my grandchildren

Jordan, Jake, Tyler, Joshua, and Emma

ACKNOWLEDGMENTS

I want to thank Sandy Mayes, one of the *Raven*'s crew members, who kept an extensive file of newspaper articles, pictures, some film footage, and, above all, a diary of the events that occurred during the voyage. These sources allowed me to refresh my memory and to record this remarkable story.

I also want to thank Diane Morriss, of Sono Nis Press, for having the courage to take on this project, and John Eerkes-Medrano and Audrey McClellan, my editors, for having done such a fabulous job of fine-tuning the manuscript.

I further want to point out that in respect to the crew of the *Raven*, in some cases I have found it necessary to change their names—to protect the guilty.

There are many tales of ghost ships. Nearly all of them involve the mysterious disappearance of crew and passengers. In all these tales, the cause of the misfortune is unknown. Sometimes the disappearances are attributed to the Bermuda Triangle, but more often than not a ghost is blamed.

In none of these occurrences was there a passenger or a member of the crew available who could explain what had happened on the ships. The reasons for their demise are therefore based on theory and conjecture.

I've always found these tales interesting to listen to and fascinating to read. However, being by nature a skeptic, I'd always taken the paranormal explanations with a grain of salt—until I became involved with a sailing ship we called the *Raven*.

The *Raven* turned out to be a ship doomed to bring misfortune to those who sailed in her. Not being aware of her mysterious background or her destiny, I was to become yet one more victim of the ghost that apparently possessed her.

Chapter One

I became involved in the *Raven*'s strange history because of an idea that occurred to me when I was anchored in a bay off Thetis Island, British Columbia, in 1971. I was the owner and operator of a sailing school known as the Vancouver Academy of Sailing, based in Fisherman's Cove in West Vancouver. The academy had a number of twenty-three-foot sailing boats and several instructors. We taught sailing, seamanship, and navigation to novices, most of whom were adults.

I also had a fifty-five-foot yawl called *Anywhere*. This boat was used for longer trips, mostly weekend excursions with students beyond the beginner's level. But on this occasion I had ten teenagers on board. They were the children of well-to-do families who had signed on for a cruise that was to last one week.

We had started the cruise from our base in Fisherman's

Cove, where the boat was moored. From there we sailed through Howe Sound and worked our way up the Sunshine Coast to Desolation Sound.

We had good weather, with favourable winds, and the kids were enjoying the trip. After leaving Desolation Sound, we crossed the Strait of Georgia and explored the Gulf Islands. Late in the afternoon, near the end of the voyage, we decided to spend the last night of the journey at the anchorage off Thetis Island. The next day we would cross the Strait of Georgia once again to return home.

It was a balmy day when we entered the bay and dropped the anchor. The tranquil waters soon tempted the kids to take a plunge over the side. While they were frolicking in the water, our cook, Marguerite, started to prepare dinner. Meanwhile, I watched the kids from the cockpit and launched the dinghy, just in case it was needed.

I noticed another group of kids arriving on the shore. They entered the water nearby and started to play water polo, supervised by a man who stood on the shore and watched them closely. Before long, our kids spotted the game in progress and swam toward the others. I couldn't hear what they were saying, but it soon became clear that our kids were being invited to join in the game.

I decided to investigate and climbed into the dinghy. With a few strokes of the oars, I arrived at the shore close to where the man was standing.

"Wow, it's hot. A perfect day for a water game," I said.

"You can say that again," he replied.

After introducing ourselves, we started a conversation. Robert explained that his kids were considered "underprivileged" and needed help because of emotional disturbances or other problems. They were under the supervision of the Department of Social Services and were attending a wilderness camp. It was hoped that this activity would bring them some benefit. Most of them came from families that were poor or had other problematic backgrounds.

I wondered about Robert's comments. My kids came from completely different circumstances. They were privileged, and their families could afford to put them on a nice yacht for an enjoyable cruise.

I watched the two groups frolicking in the water—my kids and his kids, the privileged and the underprivileged. They seemed to mix well and had no problem getting along with each other.

Soon the game came to an end. Some of the kids swam to the shore for a rest.

"Okay," Robert called to the others, "it's time to come out of the water. Let's take a break."

"If your kids are interested," I said, "why don't we invite them onto my boat for a visit?"

"Are you sure? I know they'd like that."

"Of course," I said. "My kids can show them around."

By this time, several of them had arrived on the shore. Robert turned toward them and said, "We're invited on board that yacht. Want to go and have a look?"

There was no question about their answer. The kids on shore immediately went back into the water and started swimming toward our boat. Soon the others who were still in the water followed. Robert and I climbed into the dinghy and sped toward the boat, beating the swimmers by a few minutes.

Before long all the kids were on board, my kids showing and explaining to the others the gear and various components necessary to make the boat operational. Marguerite came up from below with glasses of lemonade, which were eagerly accepted and quickly emptied.

The visitors had been aboard for well over an hour when Robert decided it was time for them to return to camp. Reluctantly, the kids said goodbye to their new-found friends and swam back to shore.

I ferried Robert back in the dinghy. When he stepped on shore, he shook my hand and said, "This has been an interesting experience. Thanks very much for inviting us on board. My kids really enjoyed it."

"It was interesting, wasn't it?" I replied. "Two groups from totally different backgrounds, and they got along so well with each other."

"I think your boat had a lot to do with that," Robert said as he waved goodbye.

That next day, while sailing back to our home port, I kept thinking about those kids. I thought of their happy faces, their interest and fascination with the boat's equipment. To no one in particular I said, "This is what they need—a trip on a sailboat!" Sailing would allow them to use and appreciate the forces of nature, the sea, the wind. It would give them an incentive to explore and enjoy the good things in life—distant horizons, beautiful coves and bays, the wonders of the stars in the sky at a remote and quiet anchorage. Meanwhile, they might experience the camaraderie that exists among the boaters they meet along the plotted course.

Little did I know that my encounter with these children

would eventually lead me to purchase the *Raven* and result in one of the strangest experiences I have ever had.

Chapter Two

The *Anywhere* was docked, and my passengers had gone home. I was scrubbing and cleaning the boat, making her ready for her next trip. While doing these chores, I kept thinking about our encounter with those kids on Thetis Island.

A plan had started to form in my mind. I looked in my Daytimer, which showed my schedule of upcoming trips. It was now the middle of July. In August, there were three weeks during which the *Anywhere* would be idle—nothing planned, no trips scheduled. This was the slow part of the season; most people were on holidays. When I was back home, I picked up the phone and called a woman who had been one of our adult students. She was a social worker employed by the provincial government.

"I have a question," I said when she answered. "I wonder if

you could find me ten kids who are in your program and badly in need of a break."

"What for?" she said.

"I want to take them on a one-week cruise on the *Anywhere*."

"They can't afford that. Are you crazy?"

"No, no, you misunderstand," I said. "It won't cost them anything. I just want to give them a good time. I have a plan. I want to know if it will work. I think a trip on a sailboat would be good for them."

"What kind of plan?"

"A plan to help these kids, to teach them to sail. I think it will be to their benefit. If it works, maybe we can do it on a regular basis."

"Oh, wow! Let me get back to you."

Two hours later my phone rang. It was the social worker. "I've discussed your plan with some of my colleagues. We've got at least thirty kids who would qualify and who could really use such an adventure. I've also mentioned your plan to a member of the Lions Club. He's pretty certain that if you take these kids on a boat trip, their organization will donate all the food."

That was good news. Food was a big issue, and a large part of the expense. This would make my plan much easier to manage. The same evening, the Lions Club confirmed that it would look after the food supply. But I couldn't handle thirty kids— there was no room for that many people on the boat. I wrestled with this problem for a while and then decided that, rather than make the difficult decision of selecting ten kids out of the group of thirty, I would split them into three groups of ten and organize three trips, each lasting five days.

Then I met with the social worker.

"I hope you realize what you're getting yourself into," she said. "Some of these kids are real troublemakers. They resent authority, they're unsociable, and they may not even get along with each other."

I took her comments and advice to heart and started to write out a curriculum, a manner in which I thought my plan might work. I figured that the project had the best chance of success if the kids were challenged to make it successful; in other words, if they wanted to go sailing, it was up to them to make the vessel operational. After all, a ship would not be able to sail unless everyone who crewed on her co-operated. I also thought it best if I was not to be regarded as their enemy, the guy who punished them for wrongdoing, so I set up a plan that I thought would give them the burden of responsibility and authority. They would select and vote for what I called "the ship's council." If anyone did not follow the agreed-upon rules, they would be called before the ship's council, which, if it found that person guilty, would deliver a verdict. That way, the culprit could only blame the people he or she had personally elected.

By the middle of August, it was time for the first voyage. The food supplies had been delivered and were being stowed away when ten kids, six boys and four girls, arrived on board. Marguerite, who had volunteered to cook and help out, took the girls into the forward cabin, where there were four berths. The boys were berthed in the main cabin, where there were three berths on each side. Marguerite was also a registered nurse and an experienced sailor. She and I occupied the berths in the pilothouse. From there we had a good view of the lower cabins and could monitor the goings-on. After the kids had settled in, I asked everyone to come into the cockpit, where they sat down on the seats while I stood in the middle to get their attention.

"Okay," I said. "Welcome aboard this fine ship. I hope you're looking forward to what I think will be one of the best times in your life. We're going for a cruise, and you are the ones who are going to sail this vessel. From now on, you are all sailors, and soon you will be experienced sailors. There are a few things to learn, but you all look to me to be pretty smart people, so it shouldn't take you long to catch on. To make this boat sail takes a co-operative effort. Each one of us will have a job to do. If we all do what is expected, then this boat will take us anywhere we want to go. That's why her name is *Anywhere*. I'm sure that by now you've seen her name painted on the bow. However, if even one of us doesn't do what is required, then this ship will not move and she stays tied up alongside the dock."

To my surprise, the kids were all paying close attention to my words. So far, so good, I thought.

"We have a few rules," I continued. "They are not hard to follow, but nevertheless they are important. We do not wear shoes. Bare feet only! This gives you a better grip on the decks and will prevent you from slipping and possibly falling overboard. It's also easier on the varnish, which, as you can see, is in pretty good shape. In any event, the weather is nice and warm, so you won't need socks and shoes. The second rule is we never fight with each other. If there is a difference of opinion it can be resolved with a discussion. Each evening, when we're anchored, we can have talks about our differences. Also, swearing and nasty comments are not allowed. Other rules: our water supply is limited, so don't leave the tap running when you're not using it. We can hear when someone uses water because it starts the pump running. In regard to the toilets, I'll show each one of you how they work but, basically, don't put anything in the toilet that hasn't gone through your stomach first."

This last announcement was met with a lot of laughter.

"Yes!" I added. "This is very important, because a plugged toilet is a nasty problem to fix. Another important thing is, we don't throw *anything* into the water. That causes pollution and hurts the fish and other creatures that live in the sea."

I waited a moment to let these things sink in. I still had my crew's undivided attention. "Anyone who doesn't follow these rules will receive an appropriate punishment to be determined by the ship's council. The council will consist of three crew members selected by you, and each day we'll appoint a new council selected by you. Since the boys outnumber the girls on the boat, we'll have one girl and two boys in each council."

The kids began to talk, point, and look at each other. The conversation became intense.

"Now is as good a time as any," I interrupted. "I'll give you twenty minutes to discuss this, and then you have to select the council."

I turned away and went below, where Marguerite was busy organizing the food supplies.

"That went pretty well," she said. "You had their undivided attention. Here." She handed me a cup of coffee. "Have a cup and relax while they're making up their minds."

I sat down in the main cabin, sipping my coffee while listening to the voices in the cockpit. It would not be an easy task for them to choose a council, since several of the kids didn't even know each other. Yet there was a debate going on, though interrupted by a lot of giggling. They were obviously in good spirits.

I looked at my watch; it was time for results. I gave my

empty cup to Marguerite and climbed the companionway ladder to the cockpit. I could tell that decisions had been made.

"Well," I asked, "who are the chosen ones?"

Two boys and a girl stood up. "We are," they said in chorus. I knew them as Fred, Mark, and Jane.

"Was this a unanimous decision?" I asked, looking around at the others.

"Pretty well," one of them answered. "It wasn't that important anyhow, because they'll be on the council for only one day. Tomorrow there will be three others, so most likely all of us will get a turn."

"Quite so," I remarked, thinking with satisfaction that this was the purpose of doing it this way.

For the next few hours I explained some of the technicalities of sailing—what certain things were called, and how they worked. "That rope is used to hoist a sail. It is called a halyard. That rope trims the sail. It is called a sheet. This is the boom, and that is the gaff. This is the mainsail, that is the mizzen sail, and there, at the front of the boat, which is called the bow, are the headsails, which include the staysail, the jib, and the flying jib. The left side of the boat is called the port side, and the right side is called starboard."

"Why are they called the port and starboard side?" one of the boys asked. "Why not left and right?"

"That's a good question," I answered. "There's a bit of history involved here. A long time ago, boats had no rudders. Instead, they used a paddle or an oar, a kind of wooden board that was lashed to the side of the boat near the stern, the aft end of the boat. Since most people are right-handed, that board was lashed to the right-hand side of the boat. It therefore became known as the steering-board side, which eventually became the starboard side. When coming alongside a dock in a port, in order to not crush the steering board between the dock and the hull of the boat, one had to go along the dock with the left side, which became known as the port side."

I was pleased to see this explanation received with interest. Then I divided the kids into groups, some for handling the headsails, some for the mainsail, and some for the mizzen sail. We partially hoisted each sail and then lowered and furled it again. After spending several hours going through the motions to make the kids understand what was required, it was time for lunch.

As they were eating, I observed my newly acquired crew. They all seemed to be enjoying themselves and were getting along with each other. They ranged in age from twelve to fifteen. The girls stayed close to each other, forming their own little group, as did the boys. However, one boy kept to himself. He didn't seem to mix or interact with the others. I had noticed earlier, on deck, that he always kept away from them. He had been quiet and sort of remote. Now I noticed him sitting quietly on the deck aft of the cockpit, eating his lunch. While the others were talking among themselves, he did not participate in the conversation. He was a fourteen-year-old, and his name was Jimmy. The social worker had given me a bundle of papers that provided me with some information about the kids: their names, age, and a bit about their backgrounds. Jimmy's sheet said that he was a loner, quiet, shy, and easily intimidated. He seemed to lack self-confidence. I thought I'd better keep an eye on Jimmy.

When lunch was over I stood up. "Before we get under way,

we need to tidy up. You two," I said pointing at two boys, "will be on galley detail for today, which means that you gather the dishes, take them below, and wash them in the sink."

"But that's a girl's job!" one of the boys said.

"No, not on a ship. Here we are all equal. Boy or girl makes no difference. We all do the same tasks—whatever's necessary."

"Hurray!" one of the girls applauded.

"So, let's get on with it. Today you two do the dishes. Tomorrow there will be two others. When you're done and the galley is shipshape, come on deck to help us sail the boat."

Without further ado, the twosome started gathering the cutlery. The others followed me on deck. The engine was started, the mooring lines were cast off, and we got under way. After motoring out of the harbour, I turned the boat into the wind and, with Marguerite steering, guided the kids through hoisting the sails. It took awhile, but eventually all the sails were up.

There was only a light breeze, just perfect for our first effort. The boat heeled slightly, picked up a bit of speed and took us on our way, gently plying the waters of Howe Sound. The kids were ecstatic, waving at other boats as we passed. A ferry leaving Horseshoe Bay crossed our path, well ahead of us. The kids waved at it, yelling with enjoyment as our boat heaved and rolled when the waves created by the ferry reached us.

"I need a helmsman," I said. "Someone to steer. How about you, Jimmy? Come here, and I'll show you how to do it."

Hesitantly, Jimmy stepped into the cockpit.

"Okay, this is what you do. Stand here and grab the tiller. When you push this way the boat turns to starboard, and when you push that way the boat turns to port. See?"

The *Anywhere* had been built in Vancouver by Elliot Shipyards in 1929, and although it was somewhat unusual these days for a boat of her size, she had a tiller instead of a wheel. This tiller was actually a good example of her well-crafted construction. It was a curved, naturally grown section of an arbutus tree, the remarkable evergreen that is native to our west coast.

Jimmy grabbed the tiller while I held onto it as well. I moved it to port and then to starboard. "Got it? Now, keep it on course. Just keep heading for that point of land over there. See it? That's Gambier Island."

The other kids were watching as Jimmy took control of the helm.

"Do we get a turn at that too?" one of them asked.

"Of course," I replied. "You'll all learn how to operate this vessel. Once Jimmy gets the hang of it, it will be his job to teach the next person."

Jimmy looked at me doubtfully.

"Don't worry," I said, "you can do it. Pretty soon you'll be an experienced helmsman."

I left him at it and went onto the foredeck, watching him from the corner of my eye. Some of the other kids had moved close to Jimmy, watching him and the approaching point of land on Gambier Island. They were talking to him, asking what it felt like, how heavy it was to push the tiller. Jimmy seemed to loosen up as he answered their questions. Good, I thought. This might give him something to brag about.

During the rest of the day we made several sail changes: sails up, sails down. We went through the motions of tacking and jibing, sailing upwind, sailing downwind, just to make the kids familiar with the various tasks necessary to operate the boat.

Eventually we anchored in Centre Bay, where we had dinner and spent the night.

During most of the manoeuvres, Jimmy had been at the helm and had done a good job. Later in the day he had passed on his skills to another crew member, but in the eyes of the other kids, Jimmy was the expert. That night I noticed him in a discussion with several of them, still talking about steering the boat. He looked a lot better—more confident, more cheerful, and much more a part of the crew. The little experiment seemed to have worked.

The five-day cruise went smoothly, without notable incidents. One thing I found amazing was the judgment of the ship's council. A peculiar thing happened on the third day of our voyage. On no other day had an incident required interference, but now we had a problem. There was a small fridge in the pilothouse. It contained beverages, which were available for anyone who was thirsty. One boy, Tommy, was in the habit of taking a soft drink from the fridge without closing the door properly. Several times I had mentioned to the kids that it was important to close that door because otherwise, when we rolled or heeled, the contents would spill out. Also, it was a waste of electricity and might drain the batteries. But for some reason Tommy always left the door open. That evening I announced that I was making a complaint to the ship's council and would ask them to deal with the problem.

The council agreed, and the session was started. The three members took their place at the centre of the table, and the culprit was seated opposite them. All the others stood close by, watching attentively while making remarks and sniggering. Some of them even booed the accused.

"Quiet," said Mary, one of the councillors. "Court is in session."

Marguerite and I were fascinated by the reaction of the kids and the attention they paid to what all of them clearly thought was a serious issue but, at the same time, great entertainment.

One of the councillors asked, "Why do you refuse to close the door of the fridge?"

"I don't know. I just forget, I guess. What's the big deal, anyhow?" Tommy answered with a smirk.

His answer received a loud cheer from the bystanders.

"Quiet!" Mary said again, this time banging her fist on the table.

Marguerite and I looked at each other. "Wow," she whispered to me. "They are taking this seriously."

"*What's the big deal?*" one of the other councillors exclaimed. "The big deal is that it causes the contents to roll out of the fridge, and it's against the rules!"

"So what are you going to do about it?" one of the bystanders asked, laughing.

Mary, who appeared to have taken charge, looked at her fellow councillors. "We will have a verdict in fifteen minutes. Court is adjourned." With this, she stood up and motioned to the other councillors. The two boys followed her into the forward cabin.

"If I didn't know any better, I would've thought she had legal training," I whispered to Marguerite. "Wasn't that amazing?"

But the big surprise was yet to come. When the trio came out of the cabin and seated themselves back at the table, Mary stood up and said, "This is the verdict: your punishment is that from now on, you are no longer allowed to close the door of the fridge. Every time you take something out of it, you must leave the door open."

I couldn't believe what I was hearing. How did they come up with that idea? It didn't make any sense; it was the complete opposite of what this was all about. I noticed that the other kids were also puzzled. However, I decided not to say anything and figured I would observe, and then deal with, whatever problem came up when it was necessary to do so.

As it turned out, the kids proved that they think differently than adults and were able to come up with original ideas. Tommy now decided that he didn't want the other kids to know when he had been into the refrigerator. I once spotted him sneaking into the pilothouse, looking around to make sure no one saw him, and quickly grabbing a soft drink. Then he carefully closed the fridge door. He even grabbed the door handle and pulled on it to make certain it was properly closed. Then he left the pilothouse, pretending that nothing unusual had taken place. It was an astonishing discovery for me. I realized I could learn a thing or two from these kids.

We had wonderful weather during the entire trip and finished the five-day cruise with all the crew regretting that it had ended. One thing I was happy to notice was that Jimmy had turned into a different person. He no longer separated himself from the others, and he was much more talkative and sociable.

The next two trips also went well, and at the end of each journey there were tears with fond goodbyes and good fellowship among the groups. Several of the crews also returned to revisit the boat long after their journeys were completed. Often I'd find a couple of them helping with the varnishing and the general upkeep of the *Anywhere*. As far as they were concerned, this was their vessel. Many of them retained that bond for several years.

To me, it was clear that the experiment had been successful. The change in the kids from the time they first came on board to the conclusion of the trip was remarkable. The experience left me with a renewed desire to do more for these kids, and for others like them. As far as I was concerned, getting them on board a sailing vessel was the way to go!

Chapter Three

Having been born in Holland, descended from a long line of seagoing ancestors, I developed an early passion for sailing. When I turned eight, I was presented with a sailing canoe that had been built in my grandfather's shipyard. My father had a sailboat, and our family usually spent weekends and vacations sailing the North Sea and Holland's many lakes and waterways. After attending the Merchant Naval Academy in Amsterdam, I served for several years in the Dutch and later the British merchant navy as a deck officer, roaming the seas and oceans.

My brother had emigrated to Canada, and in 1957 I decided to follow him. I ended up in Calgary, where he had settled. Being far from the sea, I had no choice but to get involved in a landlubber's career. In Calgary I met and married Elise, another immigrant from Holland, and we were blessed with two beautiful daughters, Michèle and Karen. Anxious to become successful, I worked hard and was lucky enough to achieve a good position, managing the western division of a large company. But I still yearned to be close to the ocean. This resulted in our decision in 1968 to move to Vancouver, where we started the sailing school. We had purchased the *Anywhere* while residing in Calgary but used her only occasionally, mainly on the odd weekend. We were now able to use her more frequently, and during our initial move to Vancouver she served us well as a live-aboard until we bought a house in West Vancouver.

Owning the *Anywhere* led us to become acquainted with Les Alfreds, who operated the Jib Set, a well-established sailing school in Vancouver. We often used our boat in the Jib Set's programs. This led us to start our own sailing school in 1969, although we stayed involved in the activities of the Jib Set. The school was successful, and we enjoyed the camaraderie with the adult students. But the experience I had just had with these kids gave me a lot to think about. Maybe *this* was what I should be doing: helping these kids, doing something really worthwhile.

I believed there were several important advantages to taking them on boat trips rather than sending them to a wilderness camp. They were classed as needy and were somewhat looked down upon by the rest of society. Most of them lacked self-esteem because everything appeared to have been against them: they were underprivileged, they had not had the good things that were awarded to the lucky ones, or things had gone wrong for other reasons. I thought they needed a boost, an opportunity to become the envy of others, to make them feel privileged. What better way to do this than by having them take a cruise on a yacht or ship, something that was usually possible only for the privileged? That would make them privileged as well and might give them self-confidence, which they needed badly. By contrast, wilderness camps, which are considered an activity for troubled people, associated them with that "looked down upon" group.

Also, after returning from a wilderness camp, the kids would return to their old environment where all their troubles had started, whereas with a boat cruise, a connection remained. Unlike a wilderness camp, which is located in a remote area, the boat was within their reach. The crew could return to it and work on it, and thereby reconnect with the friends they had made earlier. This had already been proven during the few trips we had done. Several of the kids kept returning, happily repeating tales of their journey, reminiscing about the good times they had enjoyed while under sail. Furthermore, the operation of a boat was a co-operative effort; it made the crew members relate to each other. They would pitch in to make things work, just as in normal society.

I started writing a manual, a guide to how the project was to be operated, keeping the idea of the ship's council and outlining the duties and manner of training. From time to time I discussed my ideas with my friend the social worker. The superintendent of the Department of Social Services was interested too and encouraged me to pursue my proposal. Also, Elise, who had been doing all the administrative work for our sailing school, fully supported the idea.

It had become clear that we would need a larger vessel, which could accommodate larger groups of kids. Ten at a time was not enough, especially considering that there were an estimated 65,000 kids under the direct supervision of the Department of Social Services.

I started to research the market and found a boat in the Bahamas that was for sale and might be suitable. The boat was a schooner-rigged Alden, a vessel known for its attractive and seaworthy design. This one was eighty feet long and engaged in the charter business. It had accommodation for twenty-four passengers. I phoned the owner, who told me that the vessel was in excellent condition.

At the same time, I received a letter from the Department of Social Services, advising me that there was a problem with my proposal. The Vancouver Academy of Sailing was not a non-profit society and was therefore not suitable for working with the department. The department suggested that I contact a suitable society—and mentioned the name of a potential candidate—to find out if it was interested in incorporating the project into its operation and acting as liaison with the department. Also, the proposal had to be approved by a psychiatrist.

I immediately called the non-profit society mentioned in the letter and made an appointment with some of its officials. A few days later, I met with two of them. Their society was very much involved in the rehabilitation and welfare of needy children, and they appeared to be interested in my project. The two gentlemen listened closely as I explained the whys and hows of my project. After a couple of hours of answering questions, I gave them my paperwork. They said they were very interested; they would review the material and get back to me soon. We shook hands and I left their office.

I thought the meeting had gone well and foresaw a good outcome. While waiting for the verdict, I boarded a plane for Nassau to take a look at the yacht that was for sale.

Chapter Four

Although the long flight was tiring, I arrived in Nassau in good spirits. I was looking forward to seeing the boat. As soon as I arrived, I found a phone in the airport and called the boat's owner, who told me where she was. He was unable to meet me there because he had other things to do, but he assured me there would be someone on board who could show me around. I picked up my luggage and found a taxi to take me to the boat. The marina was almost directly opposite a hotel, so I decided to check in there first. I quickly had a shower and changed my clothing to something more appropriate to the tropical climate, which had hit me as soon as I stepped out of the airplane. Feeling refreshed, I found my way back to the marina.

When I reached the gangway that led to the docks, I spotted what had to be the boat I was looking for. Yes, there she was!

I hastily walked toward her, but when I stood beside the boat on the dock, it soon became clear that I was looking at a disaster. The boat was in terrible shape. Her decks were obviously rotten, and to hide this they had been overlaid with linoleum. The cabin sides were also rotten. All this was clearly visible from where I was standing.

Just then a man stuck his head out from below. He introduced himself as the boat's captain.

"Are you the fellow from Canada?" he said with some enthusiasm.

"Yes," I answered reluctantly.

"Ah, the owner told me that you were coming."

"He told me this boat was in excellent shape, but from what I can see, it doesn't look very good. Clearly the decks are in bad shape and, by the way, that linoleum covering looks awful. What the hell is going on?"

The man started to laugh. "He told you this boat is in excellent shape? Ha! Far from it. It needs major work, and he knows it. I've told him that several times, but he doesn't want to spend any money on her. It's one of our constant disagreements. I've already told him that if he doesn't fix this boat, I'm leaving. It's becoming dangerous to sail in her. Too bad," he added, shaking his head in disappointment. "Once, this was a spectacular vessel. But she's been badly neglected."

"Well," I said, "no sense looking any further. You've just confirmed what I've already observed."

"Yeah," he said. "That's why he wants to sell her. To get rid of her."

"But not to me," I answered. I returned to the hotel, called a taxi, and went to the owner's home.

I was angry with him. He had told me that the boat was in excellent condition. Since the problems were so obvious, why had he lied to me and made me travel all the way from Vancouver to Nassau? For nothing! I knocked on his door, and when he opened it I told him who I was.

"Oh, it's so good to meet you," he said. "Please come in."

"No," I said, "no need for that. I just want to know why you said the boat was in excellent condition, when obviously it's in very bad shape."

"In bad shape?" he said sheepishly.

"Yes. Don't tell me you didn't already know that."

"Oh well, you know, maybe she does need a little work, but that's normal."

"A little work? The deck structure is completely rotten. You call that a little work? I haven't even looked at the hull, but judging from the condition of her decks, I don't think that will be much better."

Embarrassed, he stared at me, not uttering a sound.

"I just want to know," I continued, "why you lied to me and made me come all this way. For what?"

He remained silent. I raised my arms desperately into the air, then angrily turned around and returned to the waiting taxi.

The short drive back to the hotel gave me plenty of time to fume. I figured that, most likely, the owner of the boat had hoped he could sell his boat to some inexperienced victim who could be conned into believing that she was in good shape.

Back at the hotel, I was still frustrated. Not knowing what else to do, I decided to go for a walk. The hotel was close to a bridge that led across to a small piece of land known as Paradise

Island, so I walked over the bridge to the island. There I noticed some interesting vessels tied up in the marina. None of them were the size I was looking for, but I wanted to take a closer look. One vessel, a sturdy ketch about fifty-six-feet long, caught my eye. She was called *Keewatin* and appeared to be well maintained. As I stood on the dock, taking in her nice lines and sturdy rigging, a man came up from below.

"Hi," he said. "Visiting our beautiful island?"

"Yes. I came here looking for a boat. But it turned out to be a pile of junk."

"That's too bad. Which boat were you looking at?"

When I filled him in on the details, he nodded his head. "I know that boat, and I know it's in really bad shape. A pity we didn't know each other. I could've warned you and saved you the trip."

As we continued our conversation, he introduced himself as Ron Turner, an engineer and marine surveyor, and a resident of the Bahamas. In his spare time, he chartered his yacht. "As a matter of fact," he said, "I have a charter starting tomorrow, and I could use an extra hand. You're here now anyhow, so why don't you come on the charter with us? We'll be cruising the Bahamas, and since we'll be visiting various anchorages and marinas . . . who knows? You might find a boat that catches your fancy. What exactly are you looking for?"

The idea of joining Ron on the charter sounded exciting, so I immediately accepted the offer. Then I told him the sort of vessel I was looking for, and the purpose for which it was to be used.

He listened attentively and invited me to meet his family. As he drove us to his house, he suddenly said, "You know, there's a boat tied up in the harbour that may be exactly what you're looking for. And I've heard that she's for sale."

"Really! What type of vessel is it?"

"Large—over a hundred feet, a converted Baltic trader."

That got me excited. Most Baltic traders were built in Denmark. They were sailing cargo vessels, designed for carrying lumber and other general cargo to and from ports on the North Atlantic Ocean and the Baltic and Arctic seas, especially Scandinavia, Finland, Poland, and Russia. Known for their rugged construction, they were capable of carrying heavy loads while dealing with rough sea conditions. All of them were of a similar design that dated back to the end of the nineteenth century.

"She arrived here recently," Ron continued. "I'll tell you what. It's almost dinnertime, so let's go on to my home. We'll have dinner, and after that I'll take you to the harbour and we can take a look at her."

When we arrived at Ron's house, he introduced me to his wife and four-year-old son. Sonja was the complete opposite of her husband. Ron, although friendly, was a man of serious composure and with little patience for idle talk, whereas Sonja welcomed me with lots of chatter, as if I were an old friend. She was a pretty, dark-haired woman who, while preparing dinner with a smile, joined in the conversation and told several funny anecdotes about their charter experiences with the *Keewatin* and their life in Nassau.

Over dinner, we discussed the upcoming charter. Sonja would do the cooking; I would help Ron with running the boat. The charter was for a group of six people—three couples. Ron's little son would be joining us as well.

After dinner, Ron and I got into his car and drove to see the Baltic trader. I could hardly wait.

When we arrived, I saw this huge vessel, the *Raven*, tied up to a dock. She was a gaff-rigged ketch, about 140 feet in total length and 110 feet long at her waterline, a massively constructed vessel, with a broad beam of over twenty-four feet, and heavy bulwarks surrounding her decks. No way could a child accidentally fall overboard.

The boat appeared to be in good shape. On the aft section, on a slightly raised deck, was a separate wheelhouse. Otherwise, the decks were mainly flush, with lots of room for the crew to move about and tend to their duties. All the rigging was of heavy quality. The halyards were fitted with block and tackle, no winches, which was perfect for a large crew with willing hands. If ever there was a vessel suitable for my purpose, the *Raven* was it.

If I had known then what lay waiting for us deep within the confines of this ship, I would have turned the other way right then and there. But not possessing extrasensory perception and not being able to see into the future, I studied this fabulous-looking sailing vessel with great delight.

Ron and I spotted two young men aboard. They introduced themselves as Kevin and Chris and said they were part of the ship's crew. We asked if they knew whether the *Raven* was for sale. She was, they said, but the owners were not available and wouldn't be arriving for another week. They had no further details regarding price or any other information, but they invited us on board to take a look around.

The interior of the *Raven* also turned out to be exactly what I was looking for. Kevin and Chris told us that she had been built in Denmark as a cargo ship and had been converted by previous owners into a pleasure vessel. Like most Baltic traders, the *Raven* would originally have had no structural bulkheads in her hold, allowing more room for cargo. Instead of bulkheads, the hull was stiffened with an inner layer of heavy planking, creating a double hull. During the *Raven*'s conversion, the spacious cargo hold had been changed into accommodation. There were several separate cabins, a large main saloon, a big galley with a separate pantry, and lots of space, with room to install more berths if needed.

The inside was nicely finished with a cozy, old-fashioned, all-hardwood interior that suited the ship. Decorations mounted on the varnished bulkheads and walls included pictures of old sailing ships, a sculpture of a pirate's head (one eye covered with a patch), and imitation flintlock pistols and swords—a true pirate ship interior.

In the aft section of the ship, under the pilothouse, was the skipper's cabin, also large, with room to spare. There were two entrances, one to the main area and one to the skipper's cabin, and several escape hatches—again, very important for my purpose. There was a separate entrance to the engine room, which was located between the skipper's cabin and the main accommodation. The space had full headroom, and the engine was a large three-cylinder, air-start, Alpha One diesel—one of those reliable, slow-turning engines coupled to a shaft with a variable-pitch propeller.

This was 1971, well before the days of VHF radios, computers, GPS, and other electronic navigation devices. But for those days, the ship was well outfitted. She was equipped with radar, two-way AM and single-sideband radios for communication, a radio direction finder, and a recording depth sounder.

As I walked through the *Raven*, I was overwhelmed with familiar feelings. I could smell the aroma of her heavy oak frames and beech planking. I felt the smoothness of her varnished cap rails, the sturdiness of her rigging, and imagined her gentle seagoing motion as I walked across her broad and stable decks. I couldn't help but be elated and impressed with my discovery.

With the excitement in my voice difficult to contain, I whispered to Ron, "This is exactly what I'm looking for."

Ron also appeared to be pleased with what he had seen. "I thought you'd say that. I agree. She looks like a wonderful vessel, and from what you've told me, she should fit your purpose perfectly."

"Yes," I said, "and your charter ends just before the owners return. So I can go with you on your yacht and talk to these people when we're back in Nassau."

Back at the hotel, I phoned home and gave Elise an update on my travels and findings. "I'll be away a little longer than I expected." I told her about my forthcoming trip on the *Keewatin* and my hoped-for meeting with the owners of the *Raven*.

"No problem," she answered. "Everything is under control here. Don't worry."

"Okay, give the girls a big hug for me, and I'll call again as soon as I return from the sailing trip. Hopefully I'll have more news by that time."

That night I was tossing and turning in my hotel bed and kept waking up thinking about the possibilities of the *Raven* and my forthcoming journey on the *Keewatin*. Maybe coming to Nassau hadn't been a wasted trip after all.

Chapter Five

When I arrived on the *Keewatin* the next morning, Ron was already there, busy stowing groceries on board. I quickly put away my suitcase and helped him move the many boxes and bags from the dock onto the boat and down into the galley. Shortly after the stuff was put away, Sonja arrived with their four-year-old, Ken. He had a little go-cart, which he promptly started to paddle around the deck area. About an hour after we'd made everything shipshape, the guests arrived: three couples with happy faces, looking forward to their adventure. After we were all introduced, the guests settled in, and their gear put away, we cast off the mooring lines and departed.

For the next five days, we cruised and explored the islands of the Bahamas. The weather was perfect, a steady breeze moving the *Keewatin* comfortably across the clear blue waters. This was my first sailing trip through the Bahamas, and I enjoyed navigating through the unfamiliar territory. There were many coral reefs, some of which we needed to avoid and others that were deep enough to allow us to continue on our course. The reefs and coral heads could easily be seen through the crystal-clear water, but we needed to keep a constant lookout to check their depth. I learned that when the reefs were a light greenish colour, they were deep enough to clear the *Keewatin*'s bottom, but when darker and somewhat brownish, they were shallow and had to be avoided.

Ken was constantly busy with his go-cart. He had his strategy down to a fine art. He would place the cart on the aft deck and then wait until the stern was lifted by a wave from a following sea, which sped him down the decks until the bow lifted. At that precise moment, he would quickly turn the cart around, and the lifting bow would speed him back to the aft deck. I was worried, because sometimes Kenny went so fast I was afraid he would be tossed overboard. Ron, though, had seen him do this many times before and did not seem concerned.

At night we anchored or tied up in one of the many bays and harbours of the islands. At every stop, I wandered through the marinas, looking at the boats, but I did not spot one that came even close to being as suitable for my purpose as the *Raven*. When we returned to the marina where Ron's boat was berthed, the guests left and we cleaned and prepared *Keewatin* for her next voyage. It had been a valuable experience for me.

I checked back into the hotel and called home. After telling Elise about my voyage, I asked her if she had heard from the non-profit society.

"Yes," she said. "There's good news and bad news. The

society has approved the plan, and it wants to go ahead with it. But their people say that twenty-five dollars per day per child is not enough. They want it raised to sixty-five dollars per day."

"What on earth for?" I replied. "It can be done for twenty-five dollars per day. Why do they want it raised to sixty-five? They aren't running the program. We are! We only need the use of their name. We're supplying the boat, the training, and everything else."

"Yes," said Elise, "but they claim that they have expenses, administration costs, and so forth."

"Oh, I get it. Sixty-five dollars is the maximum the government allows for each child under their care, so they want to take advantage of that. So much for them being a non-profit society. What a bunch of thieves," I fumed. "Well, we'll see about that. I'll get that straightened out when I return. The more it costs, the fewer the chances are that all those kids will get access to the program. Even the government might put a stop to it, or limit it, if the program becomes too expensive."

"There's one more thing," Elise said. "The psychiatrist who reviewed the program said that something like this has never been tried before. So there are no records to indicate that it will be of benefit to the kids. He also said that it is too dangerous, because they may fall overboard and drown. He feels it's too risky and there's too much liability for the government to be involved. In other words, he doesn't support the plan and recommends against it."

"What a bunch of bureaucrats!" I ranted. I could see our plan being shut down.

"That's what we're up against," Elise said. "What now?"

"I don't know. I have to think about it. In the meantime, I'm going ahead and meeting with the owners of the *Raven*. I'll get back to you."

That evening, I kept turning the situation over and over in my mind, telling myself, "There's got to be a way to do this, to get those bureaucrats to change their minds." But I had no idea how to make this happen. Meanwhile, hoping that some solution could be found, and since I was in Nassau anyway, I decided to go ahead as planned.

The next day I went to meet with the *Raven*'s owners. They explained that the vessel was owned by a group of people who had formed a company to manage the ship. For some reason, things hadn't worked out and most of the participants were no longer interested. They had decided to sell the vessel. One of the men I met was a lawyer by the name of James Agnew. He was in full charge of the group and had power of attorney to negotiate and complete all the necessary documents for a potential sale. Agnew told me that the asking price was $55,000. Even though at that time in Vancouver one could easily buy two houses for that amount of money, $55,000 seemed reasonable for a ship of this type and size. I continued with the preliminaries of making a deal.

Ron and I went through the vessel with a fine-tooth comb and could not find any reason to back off. The *Raven* was well constructed and in excellent condition. Although we didn't anticipate any problems with her underwater components—her hull, through-hull fittings, propeller shaft, rudder, and so on— we'd have to arrange for her to be hauled out of the water at the local Nassau shipyard to examine them. But I didn't want to go to that extreme until I was certain I could go ahead with the purchase. There were complications, such as the situation with the government and the non-profit society, and even though I could come up with a pretty good down payment, the remainder of the purchase price had to be financed. I told Agnew that I had to sort a few things out and would get in touch with him within the next few days. After filling Ron in on the details, I said goodbye, went to the airport, and flew home.

Back in Vancouver, I discussed our predicament with Elise and the social worker. I also contacted the representatives from the non-profit society, but they would not budge: sixty-five dollars per child per day was what they wanted for administration and overhead.

Eventually we came to a decision. The *Raven* was too good an opportunity to pass up. If necessary, we would start our own non-profit establishment, and if the government did not want to support the program, we would raise money via donations. I was certain that we could make it work somehow. Once our sympathizers saw the *Raven*, they would be convinced to jump on board with our program. After I had a long chat with my banker, he confirmed that financing would be approved.

I phoned Agnew and told him that we would go ahead. The ship was to be hauled out, and he agreed to be responsible for any deficiencies discovered by Ron's inspection. Ron and I arranged that if everything was okay, he would instruct the shipyard to make the ship ready for an extended ocean passage. The underwater seams were to be recaulked as necessary, the bottom was to be painted with antifouling paint, and they were to put a new coat of paint on the hull topsides. I wanted the *Raven* gleaming and in perfect condition.

Ron agreed to look after this, and it was understood that when I was back in Nassau I would pay him for his services.

The transfer of payment and paperwork for the sale of the boat would be completed in Nassau within the next couple of weeks. We set a date for the takeover and another date for the vessel's departure.

I was thrilled. Success was just around the corner.

Chapter Six

I needed a paying crew to help sail the *Raven* to Vancouver and to help pay for the expenses of the voyage. Elise and I figured we could make it work if we charged $1,000 per person, an amount that would include a flight to Miami, where the crew would join the *Raven*. Once we had worked out the details, I phoned the *Vancouver Sun*, our local newspaper, and placed an advertisement to run for the next two weekends. The ad read:

EMBARK ON A FANTASTIC SEA ADVENTURE
$1,000 all-inclusive buys unique course in sailing, seamanship & navigation.
BE A PIRATE FOR 2 MTHS.
Depart from Vancouver, Jan. 14th by plane, to board our 110' Baltic Ketch in Miami. Sail to exciting & colourful ports of

the West Indies, then enter the Pacific through the Panama
Canal & set course for Vancouver via Hawaii. Limited space
available. Reserve now!
Vancouver Academy of Sailing.

In the meantime, we decided that my friend Bert Mooy
would be the captain. Bert was a licensed captain who had
served in the Dutch merchant marine for many years before
coming to Canada, where he was employed in Vancouver as a
shipping agent. He and his wife, Lenny, were our best friends.
They had two daughters, Jeannette and Ingrid, who were the
same ages as our daughters and their playmates.

Bert was also an avid sailor and well experienced in operating sailing vessels. He and I had sailed together on the *Anywhere*
many times. He was a stockily built fellow of medium height,
with a round, bearded face that complemented his good mood
and happy smile. When on a ship, Bert was in his element. He
was a dedicated, serious, and well-respected ship's captain.

Elise and I would join the voyage too, but only as far as
Panama. From there we had to return to Vancouver to make
preparations for the program upon the *Raven*'s arrival. During
the voyage to Panama, I could help train the paying crew, who
by the time of our departure should be well experienced and,
under Bert's command, capable of continuing the voyage to
Vancouver. We also needed a cook and a few experienced hands
as permanent staff in addition to the paying crew.

Bert introduced me to Tom de Roos, one of his sailing
buddies. Tom was a medical doctor who volunteered to join as
unpaid crew. He was tall and lean, dark-haired, with a little,
black, well-groomed moustache. He had an optimistic and

good-natured soul and was a bit older than the rest of us. A pipe was constantly clamped between his teeth and lips. Sailing was his favourite pastime. Tom owned a thirty-foot sailboat that had his undivided attention. Whenever he was not at work in his medical practice, he was either sailing or working on his boat to keep her in top shape. A better candidate could not be found, and having a doctor aboard the *Raven* would be a valuable asset.

Another sailor who volunteered as unpaid crew was Ray Metcalf, an able hand who had accompanied us on many trips with the *Anywhere*. Ray was a single guy, about thirty, who had many friends, most of them women who owned sailboats. He was good-natured, perhaps a bit pessimistic—he often looked at the negative side of things—but he was reliable and could be counted upon.

I also placed an ad in the paper to find a cook. Unfortunately, Marguerite, frequently our cook on the *Anywhere,* was not available now because of her job as a registered nurse. Of those who responded to the ad, three drew my attention. One was the chef of a fancy hotel in Calgary, another a retired cook from the merchant marine, and the third a young man who was the cook at a ski resort. I ruled out the chef because I thought that, being used to all the fancy equipment available in an expensive hotel, he might not be happy with the simple and confined facilities of a sailing ship.

The retired merchant mariner was the obvious choice, but for some reason he was unable to obtain a passport. That ruled him out.

Last was the young cook from the ski resort. Francois was originally from Quebec and spoke with a French accent. He seemed amiable and was anxious to join us on the trip. I figured that his enthusiasm, his youth, and the fact that he was a cook at a ski resort made him a suitable prospect, so I put him on our paid crew list. In my haste, I neglected to obtain references. It turned out that he knew less about cooking than I did, which was virtually nothing. But I didn't know this until we were ready to set sail.

After the weekend ad for paying crew appeared, the phone started ringing. Within a day, every passenger berth on the ship had been booked. I cancelled the second ad because the phone kept ringing. One individual, who introduced himself as Jack Owens, arrived at my house after I had told him that we were fully booked. He had brought a couple of cases of beer as a bribe.

"Can't you fit me in somehow?" he asked plaintively. "I don't care where I have to sleep. I definitely want to come."

I'm not much of a beer drinker, but Jack's gift was an indication of his eagerness to join us on the trip. Since he was so full of enthusiasm, I went over the ship's plan and figured we could squeeze him in somewhere. So he was added to the list.

The next weekend we had a meeting with the entire crew complement—the volunteer crew, the paid crew, and the paying crew. First I explained the purpose of the trip: the boat would be used to help underprivileged children, and the fee we charged the paying crew would help cover the expense of bringing the boat to Vancouver. This prompted a lot of questions about how the program was going to work. I explained it in detail, mentioning that our initial plan to do this via a non-profit society, aided by the government, had failed and that we hoped instead to achieve our objective via donations. The group seemed to be sympathetic to the project, and several crew members said they were happy to be a part of it. I also explained that although the *Raven* was a well-outfitted and comfortable sailing ship, it was a working vessel and should not be confused with a fancy cruise ship. The crew would be expected to participate in the work, and they would be treated as crew, not as passengers. In other words, they were expected to pitch in wherever they were needed. And it would be a learning experience; as mentioned in the ad, they would be taught sailing, seamanship, and navigation.

I went on to explain some of the on-board duties and said that each of the crew would be assigned to a watch. Furthermore, we had some strict rules, such as no alcohol consumption while on watch.

"Does that mean we're not allowed to drink on board?" one of them asked.

"No, of course not," I answered, "as long as you don't drink while on duty. We can't have people impaired while on watch. That might cause accidents."

Everyone seemed to agree with what had been discussed, and all said they were really looking forward to the trip.

Then we served pastries and coffee and tea, and the group relaxed and started chatting. Engaging in some of the conversations, I thought they seemed to be a nice bunch of people.

We set a date for departure. The group would be accompanied by Joan Whiteley, a young woman who had been an enthusiastic participant in many of the *Anywhere*'s weekend trips. Eventually, because of her regular participation, she had become part of the sailing academy and had assisted us in many projects. As the travel coordinator, she would ensure that the group arrived safely in Miami, where they would join the ship.

Bert Mooy, Ray Metcalf, Tom de Roos, and Elise and I would depart a few weeks earlier and fly to Nassau. There we would make the required changes to the interior of the ship to accommodate the large crew complement that would be joining us in Miami. After the modifications, we would sail the boat to Miami to pick up the rest of the crew. This would give us and the boat a good sea trial before setting out on the long voyage. Bert, of course, would be the captain. For the short voyage to Miami, Ray, Tom, and Elise and I would be crew. Once the rest of the gang was on board, Bert as captain and Ray and Tom as mates would each be in charge of a watch. My function was to be wherever I was required, to train the new crew until we reached Panama, and share my watch with Bert when I wasn't needed somewhere else. Elise would act as purser, taking care of the domestic requirements such as helping the cook with the provisioning and menus, other household chores, and paper-work. She would work closely with Joan, who would take over these duties after Elise and I had left the ship.

There was a lot of work to be completed in a short time. We had to make all the interior modifications before the arrival of the main group. It was extremely important that the shipyard in Nassau had the boat ready upon our arrival so we could start the modifications immediately. I was in constant touch with Agnew, the vendor's representative, to ensure that everything went ahead as planned.

Eventually the big day arrived. I hadn't heard from Ron and therefore assumed that he hadn't discovered any problems with the *Raven*. As far as I knew, she was ready—painted and wait-ing for us to start the modifications.

On the evening of January 4, 1972, Bert, Ray, Tom, and

Elise and I, with our two girls, boarded the plane in Vancouver. We would make a short stop in Calgary, which allowed us to drop off our daughters; they would be staying with their grandparents, who lived in Calgary. Elise's parents met us at the airport to collect the girls. After exchanging many goodbyes and hugs, we went back to the plane and continued our flight to Nassau.

Chapter Seven

It was late the next day when we arrived. We were tired, but since no one but me had seen the ship and all of us were eager to get aboard her, we decided to go straight to the *Raven*. We loaded our luggage into a taxi and asked the driver to take us to the harbour. When he dropped us off at the dock, there was no sign of our ship. Puzzled, we wandered around the docks and looked for the *Raven*, but with no luck. Not knowing what else to do, I left the docks and walked along the road until I found a phone booth. I entered, picked up the phone, put some coins in the slot, and asked the operator to connect me with Ron Turner.

"She's still in the shipyard," he said. "There were some delays. I tried to call you but didn't get an answer. I guess you'd already left."

"What kind of delays?" I asked. "She was supposed to have

been surveyed and made ready for the voyage."

"Yes, she was. But the shipyard had to deal with an emergency on another vessel. So the haulout was delayed."

"You mean they haven't even started on her yet?"

"Yeah, that's right, but there was nothing I could do about it. On the positive side, I've finished surveying the bottom. I did that as soon as she was hauled, and everything is okay."

This delay was terrible news, but I couldn't blame Ron. It was beyond his control. Regardless, I had difficulty staying calm. Many questions went through my head. How were we going to get the boat ready? Was there enough time to get everything done before the deadline? We had to get the boat to Miami to receive the group that was scheduled to fly in from Vancouver. In despair, I hung up the phone.

"We've got a problem," I yelled to my comrades, who were now standing with their luggage at the spot where the taxi had dropped us off. "She's still in the shipyard. Let's go. We might as well walk. It's not far from here."

We picked up our luggage and started walking. When we arrived at the shipyard, sure enough, there was the *Raven*, hauled out of the water on the ways. Loud music was playing, and I could hear shouting and laughing from a large number of people gathered on her decks. There was obviously a party in progress.

Seeing a tall ladder positioned against the vessel, I climbed on board, leaving the rest of the gang waiting below on the ground. Hoisting myself over the bulwarks, I stepped on deck and made my way through the partiers in search of James Agnew. I soon spotted him, with a drink in his hand, talking to a group of people, and I pushed myself through the crowd surrounding him.

"What's happening?" I asked.

"Oh," he said, suddenly recognizing me. "I thought you wouldn't be here until tomorrow. We're having a farewell party. Come and join us."

"But," I said, "the ship was supposed to be ready to go to sea. And here she is, still in dry dock."

"Yes," he replied, "there have been a few delays. You know, after all, this is the Bahamas. We're on Island time. Things here do not always happen the way we're used to. They'll start to work on her tomorrow. We were just hauled out about four hours ago."

"Yeah, I just talked with Ron Turner and he told me the same thing," I said. "But I spoke to you about a week ago, and nothing was mentioned about this delay. Why didn't you tell me?"

"I didn't know this was going to happen. I didn't find out about it until I arrived here yesterday. I was as surprised as you are. But what's wrong with a few more days on this beautiful island?" He laughed and offered me a glass. "Here, get yourself a drink and join the party."

"No thanks," I answered. "I'll be back tomorrow. Hopefully we can straighten things out. We have lots of work to do, and time is of the essence."

I went back to the people who were waiting for me. When I told them what the situation was, Ray, our pessimist, said, "We're in big trouble. We'll never be able to get that ship ready in time. We might as well go back to Vancouver."

The others agreed that we were facing a desperate situation.

"Calm down now," I said, trying to stop the moaning and groaning. "We're all tired from the long flight. Let's check into a hotel and have a good night's sleep. Tomorrow is another day, and we can decide what to do when we're rested and in a better mood."

We checked into the hotel I had stayed at during my previous visit. It was within walking distance of the shipyard. Elise and I shared a room and, to save a few bucks, Tom, Ray, and Bert shared another.

That night I couldn't sleep. We appeared to be facing a hopeless situation. How was I going to solve this? I put my clothes back on and went outside for a walk.

The night was clear, the stars brilliant in the sky. As I was walking, I remembered a time long ago when my mother and I, during the war years in Holland, had to escape to another part of the country. We had walked for miles and miles, and when I was tired, my mother often said to me, *"Doorzetten, Jan. Nooit opgeven."* ("Persevere, Jan. Never give up.")

"No, Mom," I mumbled to myself. "I won't give up."

A plan started to form in my mind. By making a few changes, and with a bit of luck, we could still make it. Having come to a decision, I returned to the hotel and went back to bed. After some tossing and turning, I finally fell into a sound sleep.

The next morning, I explained my plan to the others. "The only real problem we have is that we might not make it to Miami in time to pick up the passenger crew. So if we reroute them to fly to Nassau instead of Miami, they can board here. That will give us an extra couple of days. I see no reason why we can't start the work while the ship is in dry dock. And providing I can get the shipyard to put in some overtime, we should still be able to get the boat ready in time. Even if we encounter some delays after she's back in the water, that won't matter, because when the rest of the group is on board, we can delay our departure. No one will object to spending a few extra days in Nassau. So let's pick up our bags and go to the *Raven* and get started. Hopefully that crowd has left the ship by now.

"If not, we'll tell them to get lost."

Chapter Eight

Everyone was confident that the new plan would work. Bert, Tom, Ray, and Elise left for the *Raven* while I stayed behind to call Joan Whiteley and let her know about the change of destination. I explained the situation to her and asked her to call the airline to make the necessary adjustments to the itinerary.

As it turned out, the new arrangements added quite a bit to the airfare—something else to be concerned about. But I had no choice. Joan assured me that she would look after everything from her end, including advising everyone of the change in plans. With a sigh of relief, I hung up the phone.

My next stop was the shipyard, where I had a talk with the manager. He confirmed what Ron had already told me: the delay was because of an emergency with another vessel. It had sprung a plank and was taking on water. I understood and agreed that, under those circumstances, they'd had no choice but to attend to the other vessel first. The manager assured me that he would see to it that the *Raven* was made ready and launched as soon as possible. He also confirmed that he and Ron had already inspected the bottom and that everything was in good shape. The work was straightforward and simple. He expected no surprises that would hold it up.

So far, so good. I went on board and found my crew already hard at work on the alterations we had extensively planned, discussed, and designed in Vancouver, using the blueprints of the ship. Now that we were aboard the real thing instead of just working with blueprints, Bert and I went over the planned alterations and made some minor changes that suited our purpose better.

The main items were the building of berths and the addition of another cabin to provide comfortable accommodation for everyone. Two berths, an upper and a lower, were to be added to the skipper's cabin on the port side. There was plenty of room for this. The main berth, on the starboard side, was a double, and it would be occupied by Elise and me. Tom, the ship's doctor, and Bert would use the newly added berths on the port side.

We all were pretty handy and capable of doing the carpentry work. All of us were used to working on boats. Even Tom had no difficulty exchanging a scalpel for a hammer or a chisel. Bert and Ray started making up a list of the materials we needed to carry out the work. There were plenty of tools, so at least that was not a problem. In the meantime, Elise started measuring the sizes of the berths to be added so that we could purchase foam pads or mattresses for them.

While all this was going on, I met with James Agnew and drew up the paperwork to sign the boat over to the Vancouver Academy of Sailing. We did this at the Dutch consulate, since it appeared to be easier and quicker to register the vessel under the Dutch flag—the flag of the Dutch Antilles, Curaçao, to be exact. Registering in Canada when we were in the Bahamas would have been a much more complicated affair. Dutch registration also seemed appropriate because Bert had a Dutch master's certificate, although this was not required at that time for captaining a pleasure or charter vessel.

With the completed paperwork in hand, I returned to the ship. While boarding, I noticed with pleasure that several of the yard's shipwrights were busy with the bottom work. Things were coming together; we'd get the *Raven* ready after all. "Thanks, Mom, for pushing me on," I said to the warm breeze that blew around me as I climbed over the bulwarks.

"All the paperwork is finished," I said to Bert, putting the documents on the saloon table. "We now own the *Raven*, and she is registered under the Dutch flag. Everything is legal and signed and sealed by the Dutch consul. These are temporary registry papers. The permanent document will be forwarded by mail. However, once we're in Canada, we'll have to change the registry to Vancouver, Canada, so that we can operate there legally. Also, the bank that's financing this vessel requires Canadian registration. But for the time being, and for the voyage home, we will be official."

"Great," Bert said, picking up the papers and looking at them. "I'd better put these away in a safe place."

"Yes, you're the captain and you'll need them when entering and clearing foreign ports. So take them. They're all yours," I said, giving him a happy slap on the shoulder. Then, changing the subject, I asked, "How is the work progressing?"

"Well, Jan, I think we've got everything figured out and are ready to get the materials. We need plywood and other lumber, nails and screws and that kind of stuff. Elise has all the measurements of the bunks, and she and Ray have already gone shopping to get mattresses. I think she also said she needed more sheets, blankets, and towels."

"We can leave that to her. It's a good thing Ray went with her, because there'll be a lot of stuff to carry. Mind you, if they're getting mattresses they'll need a truck."

Bert took me through the boat, showing me where the major changes were going to be made. In one of the larger cabins, two berths were to be added to accommodate a family of four: two adults and two children. Another large cabin would also get two more berths, to accommodate four guys who were friends and had jointly signed up for the voyage. A small, separate cabin was to be built under the stairwell that led to the decks. This was to be the space for a young couple who had signed on for the voyage. The rest of the crew would be accommodated in the remaining staterooms, which did not require alteration.

"Good," I said to Bert. "That should work out well. They should all be quite comfortable, bearing in mind that this is a working vessel and not a luxury cruise ship."

Bert handed me a list of the materials we needed. "That's a rough estimate," he said. "We will probably need more as we get going."

I looked at his notes. "I bet most of this stuff is available right here in the shipyard," I said. "I'll take this and have a chat with the yard's manager."

List in hand, I went to the yard's office. The manager glanced at the list and asked what we needed the material for. I explained that we were building more bunks and doing some other renovations.

"Look behind that shed," he said as he pointed to a shed in the yard. "Behind it is a large pile of lumber. Most of it is waste from other projects, but you may find a lot of it of use. You're welcome to take it. Screws and nails we have here—plenty of them, all sorts and sizes. As far as the sheets of plywood are concerned, we don't have any, but I can order them for you and have them delivered. They should be here by tomorrow morning."

"That's great," I said. "Thank you very much." We were in business.

I returned to give Bert the good news. From the ground, looking up at the massive hull of the *Raven*, I yelled, "B-e-r-t!"

After a few more calls, he stuck his head over the side of the boat.

"Come on down here!" I shouted. "I've got something to show you."

When Bert came down, I told him about the yard manager's suggestion. We went to the shed and found the lumber. There was a lot of useless scrap, but also many good boards of longleaf pine that would be perfect for the job. Not much useful timber grew in the Bahamas, so I guessed that most of the shipyard's lumber came from nearby Florida. We started sorting through the piles, ending up with more than we could possibly use. Rather than bringing everything on board at once, we decided to take the pieces of wood as we needed them, while the work was under way.

Just as we were about to get back on board, a truck drove up.

Elise and Ray were sitting in the cab beside the driver, and they waved at us as the truck drew nearer.

Ray jumped out first and said, "We have the mattresses."

"We were lucky," Elise said when she joined us. "These mattresses are exactly the right size, and the store had the amount that we needed. The last one they managed to find somewhere stored in the back of the building. This is much better than having to use foam pads, because now we don't have to make covers for the foam—which is a good thing, because we don't have a sewing machine."

We went to the back of the truck and started hauling the load on board. It was quite a job, especially hauling mattresses up the tall ladder. There were also boxes containing sheets, towels, and blankets. When we had stored it all neatly away, we were exhausted and decided to take a break. It was after 6:00 p.m. and getting dark, but the shipwrights were still at work. We went to a nearby restaurant and discussed our progress during dinner.

Shortly after we arrived back at the boat, two visitors climbed on board. They turned out to be Kevin and Chris, the ex-crew men I had met when I first discovered the *Raven*.

"Welcome aboard," I said to them. "Let me introduce you to the rest of the gang." After the usual shaking of hands, we went below and showed them the work in progress. They seemed interested.

Kevin and Chris were young guys, probably in their early twenties. Both were amicable and good-looking, clean-shaven, their faces tanned by the tropical sun, and their blond hair thoroughly bleached by it. Kevin did most of the talking; Chris was a bit more reserved.

"What are you guys up to?" I asked after we had seated ourselves around the large table in the main saloon. "I thought you'd gone back to the States."

"No, we like it here. Decided to stay a little longer," Kevin answered. Chris nodded in agreement.

"While you're here," I said, "unless you've other things to do, how about giving us a hand getting the ship ready? We could use a couple of extra hands." I offered them a modest sum of money for their services.

They looked at each other. "Yeah, why not," they said. "We don't have any other plans. If we could stay aboard, that would save us a hotel bill too."

"Agreed," I said. "There's lots of room until the others arrive."

Chris and Kevin told us that they had joined the ship in Spain and helped sail her to Nassau. From them we learned that the original name of the ship had been *Danebrog*. That was also the name of the Danish royal yacht, so the owners, the ones from whom James Agnew and his group had purchased the boat, had been forced to change it. They renamed the boat *Raven*.

"That's not a good omen," Ray remarked. "It's bad luck to change the name of a ship."

"Yes," Bert replied, "that's what they say. I don't like changing the name of a ship either. When we get to Vancouver, we'd better change her name back to *Danebrog*."

"Ah!" Tom said, pulling his pipe out of his mouth. "It's just superstition."

"Maybe," Ray mumbled, "but it's a bad omen just the same, especially calling her after a bird. *Raven*—not a good name for a ship. Ravens give bad karma."

"Yes, that's true," Tom said after taking a few puffs from his pipe. "According to First Nations people, ravens are mysterious birds and considered to be tricksters. The Haida, especially, have lots of tales about ravens."

"Okay, that's enough," I said, breaking up the conversation, which in my opinion was beginning to take on a depressing tone. "We now have two extra men to get the ship ready. Let's get to bed and make a fresh start in the morning."

Hiring Kevin and Chris was a good decision. They turned out to be very capable and were a big asset in carrying out the many tasks. I discussed their presence with Bert. "Those two guys know this ship well," I said. "They've been crew on *Raven* for some time and know all the idiosyncrasies and details about the engine, the rigging, and all those things that would take us a bit of time to figure out. Maybe I should ask them to stay aboard for the voyage as well. It would be good to have two experienced extra hands."

"I agree," Bert said, "but we're pretty full as it is. Where are we going to find berths for these guys? I suppose we could build two more bunks in the pantry, off the galley. It would be a bit tight, but they're young guys and probably won't mind."

"That's a possibility," I said. "But first let's find out if they're interested."

That afternoon we were sitting on deck in the sunshine, having lunch that Elise had prepared. I asked Kevin and Chris, "What are your plans after the work is finished here?"

"We don't know," Kevin said. "Haven't thought about it yet."

"How about coming with us and sailing the boat to Canada?"

They looked at each other. Kevin took a bite of his sandwich.

Chris started to move some crumbs around on his plate. Neither of them said anything. Kevin chewed and Chris kept fiddling with the crumbs.

"Well?" I asked.

Kevin put his plate down and uncomfortably shifted his position on the railing he'd been sitting on. "We can't," he said. Chris nodded in agreement.

"You can't? Why not?"

Kevin shook his head. "It's a long story, too many things have happened."

"What do you mean?"

"That's why they sold the boat," Chris said.

"Yes," said Kevin. "All of them were scared."

Their response had drawn everyone's attention. We gathered around the twosome.

"What the hell are you talking about?" said Bert.

Kevin was hesitant. "There's a ghost aboard this ship. We're convinced of it."

"A ghost?" I exclaimed. "Come on."

Tom started to laugh. "That sounds interesting. Tell us about it," he said.

"Yeah," we all said. "Let's hear it!"

"Well," Kevin said, "the people who sailed the boat from Denmark to Spain left her because they'd had a nasty experience in the Bay of Biscay. She almost sank and had to go into a shipyard there for repair. After she was repaired, our group brought the boat from Spain to Nassau. We made it, but we had some really weird experiences during our voyage. Too many strange things happened."

Having said that, Kevin turned pensive and looked into the

distance. Chris was still fiddling with the crumbs on his plate.

"What kind of strange things?" Tom asked.

This time Chris answered. "Lights would go on or off for no explainable reason. Doors to cabins were opened and closed during the night, and we saw an apparition sort of floating through the ship—many times."

"Yes," Kevin said, "that's what happened. It was creepy. I know it sounds silly, but we've had our fill of it and don't want to go through that anymore. The owners—all those people who had shares in the boat—saw the ghost as well and witnessed the same unexplainable experiences with lights and doors. That's why they wanted to get rid of the *Raven*. We were surprised that they were even willing to come aboard for the party when you arrived. But I suppose they felt, as we do, that if the ghost appears while the ship is tied to a dock, you can leave and step ashore."

I stared at them, unbelieving. A great story, but what a bunch of crap. We had stayed on board during the refit and hadn't noticed anything unusual. We certainly hadn't seen any ghost floating around. I figured Kevin and Chris must have another reason for not wanting to come with us. But they weren't going to tell us. Too bad—we could have used their help.

Later that evening, when Kevin and Chris had gone ashore to visit one of the local bars, Bert, Ray, Elise, Tom, and I talked about what we had heard. Everyone thought it was funny, except Ray, who had his doubts. He believed there was some truth in the story and that it had something to do with the name of the ship having been changed.

"I don't believe in ghosts," I said. "If anything strange happened, there's got to be a logical explanation. It's a good tale, but just to be on the safe side—and in case some of our passengers are superstitious—we'd better keep this to ourselves. We can tell them about it after they've completed the voyage." Everyone agreed, and we went to bed, anticipating another busy day of preparation.

Chapter Nine

Work on the *Raven* progressed well. The shipyard had almost completed its work, and the shipwrights were busy with the finishing touches. They had recaulked the planking seams where necessary and were reinstalling the copper sheathing that covered much of the hull's bottom. Several of the old sheets had to be replaced, but fortunately they were available at the shipyard. This plating served as a ground for the single-sideband radio and the radar, and protected the wood from being attacked by worms. Bert and I inspected the shipyard's work and were well satisfied with the result. A couple of coats of antifouling paint were yet to be applied. After that, the *Raven* would be ready to roll down the ways back into her element, the salty waters of the world's seas and oceans.

By the time we had been in Nassau for four days, the ship's

hull bottom was coated with a layer of antifouling paint and she was ready to be launched. The *Raven* shuddered and shook as the cradle on which she sat started to move down the ways. A heavy cable attached to a large winch at the top of the ways gradually released the heavy load of the boat, allowing her to slide slowly down the track toward the water. When she came to the end of the ways, the *Raven* slipped partially off her cradle and into the water, but she was not yet afloat. Her bottom was sitting on the sand, and a part of her was still stuck on the cradle.

It was high tide, and we should have been afloat. There is not much of a tide in the Bahamas—the change is at most perhaps two feet, not like the tides we are used to in Canada, where they can rise or fall in excess of fourteen feet. Maybe we had miscalculated, and the next high tide would be higher. To be on the safe side, we tied some mooring lines from the *Raven* to the pilings positioned at the end of the ways.

"While we are waiting," Bert said to me, "we might as well launch the dinghy and go ashore to get more of those supplies we need."

I agreed. We launched the dinghy, a sturdy lifeboat, and Bert and I jumped on board. Its outboard motor was still stowed away on deck, but since we had only a short distance to go, Bert picked up an oar. He started sculling and moved the vessel with good speed through the water. When I looked back at the *Raven*, I suddenly noticed she was shifting slightly from her original position.

"Stop, Bert!" I yelled. "I think she's afloat!"

Bert looked at the *Raven*. "I think you're right. She *has* moved a bit."

Now we noticed the crew, still aboard, running on the decks, tying more mooring lines to the pilings.

"How the hell is that possible?" Bert said as he turned our craft around. "The tide is going out! She should be settling onto the ground more firmly."

"Maybe the sand at the bottom has shifted," I said. This could have happened, as *Raven*'s bottom was sitting on it, thus perhaps diverting the current. "Or maybe the cradle was temporarily stuck on the rails and has now moved again."

"Or we misread the tide table," said Bert, "or that table isn't accurate."

"But the yard manager would have known that, wouldn't he?" I asked.

"Yeah. Who knows," Bert agreed as he sculled once more, this time speeding us back toward the *Raven*.

"We're afloat," Tom hissed as we climbed on board. Taking his pipe out of his mouth, he continued, with clearer speech, "We had to put some more lines on her, otherwise we might have drifted away."

"Okay," said Bert. "Let's start the engine and see if we can move her to her berth."

We manually turned the large flywheel to the right position and injected a burst of compressed air from the air tank, and the engine started with a hiss and a puff. The mooring lines were cast off, and the ship began to move. Yes, she was definitely afloat. Expertly, Bert manoeuvred the *Raven* alongside a dock where people were waiting to take our mooring lines. When the ship was firmly secured, we stopped the engine and took a moment to recover from this somewhat exciting experience.

Later I asked the manager of the shipyard if he had any idea why the *Raven* hadn't come afloat immediately after she was launched.

He scratched his head. "I have no idea," he said. "We've never had this problem before. We never pay much attention to the tide. In this case, we did check the tide table. Only because the other fellow," he said, referring to Bert, "insisted on it. The water is deep enough, even at low tide. We have launched larger ships than the *Raven*, and the tide has never been a problem. It's a real puzzle. Like I said, I have no explanation."

"Whatever the reason," I said, "she's now safely tied to the dock, so we don't have to worry about it anymore."

I didn't give much more thought to the incident. Now that the ship was back in the water, it felt a lot better. After she was launched, we regularly inspected the bilges. Sometimes a ship like this, after being out of the water for a while, takes some time to settle. It might have leaky seams until the wood has settled back into its proper shape. But there were no leaks. The *Raven* was as tight as a drum—a good sign.

With the boat afloat and alongside the dock, the work aboard was easier. No longer did we have to climb that tall ladder, and it was a much easier job to hoist heavy items on board. We could also test all the ship's systems now too.

It soon became clear that there was a problem with the refrigeration system, so we hired a technician to deal with that. Then we tried the radar and the radios, flushed the heads, filled up the water tanks; everything worked. We needed more safety gear, fire extinguishers, life jackets, and so on. Fortunately, the *Raven* had come with three large, inflatable life rafts enclosed in capsules, ready to be launched overboard in case of an emergency. The inspection tags were up to date. With these rafts and the large dinghy, or lifeboat, we could easily accommodate the entire crew that was to sail in her.

The day the balance of the crew was to arrive, we decided to rig some lights in the shrouds that would illuminate the decks. The newcomers were flying in that evening, and the lights would be a welcoming sight and would allow us to have a party on board to celebrate their arrival. We installed simple light fixtures that we purchased at a local hardware store and connected to shore power via an extension cord. For the occasion we also hired a band, a small group of locals with steel drums. Their music would add the appropriate flavour to our Bahamian location.

Elise had arranged for food and beverages to take care of the first few days. The main provisioning for the voyage would be done by the cook when he joined us.

As we awaited the newcomers, the *Raven*'s ex-crewmen, Kevin and Chris, left the ship. I tried again and again to talk them into coming with us, but they wouldn't change their minds.

"Soon you'll understand why," they said. "That ghost will reappear."

I could only shrug my shoulders and laugh. "Okay, if you want to stick to your story, so be it. Thanks, anyway, for your help!" I figured they had other plans, and suspected those plans had something to do with the two pretty girls they had brought on board a couple of times.

Chapter Ten

 Shortly after we said goodbye to Kevin and Chris, taxis began to arrive and the band started playing. It was about eight in the evening when baggage was hoisted over the bulwarks by a tired but jubilant group of people. Elise showed each party to their cabins. Drinks and hors d'oeuvres were handed out. Hands were shaken, and "Welcome aboard" was said numerous times. The newcomers looked around the ship and made themselves at home. Some were already dancing to the music.

One problem occurred. Jack Owens, the man who had practically begged me for a berth on the boat, came toward me, one arm tightly wrapped around a woman I had never seen before.

"This is Susan," he said. "She's coming too."

"What do you mean, 'She's coming too'?" I asked.

"She's coming on the trip to Vancouver. I'll pay for her passage."

"But that's impossible, Jack. We don't have the space."

"That's all right. She won't take up any space. She's with me."

It was obvious that Jack had consumed several drinks before coming aboard. Susan also seemed a bit unsteady on her feet.

"Sorry, Jack," I replied. "As I said, we can't accommodate her. We can't take any more people on the voyage."

My response made Jack angry, and when he was shown to the berth allocated to him, he said it wasn't good enough. I offered to refund his money so that he could return to Vancouver. When he declined the offer, I told him that if his behaviour didn't improve, I would insist that he take his refund and go home. Somewhat irritated, I turned around and went to look for Joan, who had been in charge of the group since its departure from Vancouver. From the corner of my eye, I noticed Jack and Susan leaving the boat.

"I'll be back later!" he yelled. We're going into town!"

I thought back to the time Jack had brought us two cases of beer to persuade us to take him on the voyage. Maybe I should have taken that as a warning.

When I found Joan, I asked her what the story was about Jack and his friend.

"Oh," she said, "that guy has been a real pain in the neck. He was almost kicked off the plane because he drank too much and made a nuisance of himself. I had to constantly drag him out of airport bars, with barely enough time to get him on the next flight. That woman, he met on the plane. He acts as if he knows her, but he doesn't—they just met. She must be some kind of floozy. They were constantly necking on the plane and making other people feel uncomfortable. I wish Jack would go away," she sighed. "He'll be trouble on the trip."

"That gives us something to think about," I replied. "Better keep a close eye on him." I was now convinced that granting him passage had been a mistake.

While the party was under way, a small freighter tied up alongside us. The ship was laden with wooden crates, which turned out to be empty tomato crates destined for one of the outlying islands, where they would be filled. After the freighter was tied up, her crew watched the party for a while and then turned in to their bunks. Their arrival did not stop the party-goers from having a good time. The festivities lasted until well after midnight.

The next day everyone, somewhat bleary-eyed, gathered around the table in the main saloon. A late breakfast was being served. They all appeared to be there, except Jack Owens. I wondered if he was still asleep. Perhaps he hadn't returned and was otherwise occupied with his new-found lady friend.

When I asked if anyone had seen Jack, one of the crew said, "Yes, he came aboard. I woke up during the night and went up on deck, and I saw him arrive. I think he was drunk. He sort of stumbled over the bulwarks, then went across the deck and climbed on board the freighter that's tied up alongside us."

"He boarded the freighter?"

"I saw him board it, but then he disappeared among those crates."

"But the freighter's no longer here. It left early this morning," I said. "Are you sure he boarded it?"

"No question about it. I'm positive."

Just to be sure, I went to Jack's sleeping quarters. They were empty. Good riddance, I thought, we can do without that one. It seemed the problem had solved itself.

About an hour later, we were all on deck when we spotted the freighter speeding back into the harbour. At first I thought it was going to pass us by, but then it altered course and seemed to be coming alongside us again. But it wasn't slowing down. As it approached us at close quarters, we saw Jack on its railing. Two men stood beside him. At the appropriate moment, he was given a firm push. The freighter increased her speed after Jack made his precarious jump, then sped away. Jack tumbled on board and sat on the deck, his legs spread wide, rubbing his eyes.

Here we go again, I thought. The culprit is back.

Later we heard his story. Jack had fallen asleep among the tomato crates on the freighter. When he woke up, the ship was at sea. In the distance he could see Nassau. He managed to climb over the crates, and while doing so was confronted by the skipper.

"Where the hell am I?" Jack yelled.

"Where the hell did you come from?" the skipper replied in turn.

When Jack told him he was supposed to be on the *Raven*, the skipper swore, went to his steering station, and turned the ship around. He called two of his crew, told them to grab Jack, and ordered them to throw him over the side as soon as they were close enough to the *Raven*.

During breakfast, we briefed everyone on the *Raven*'s present status and explained why we had rerouted them directly to Nassau instead of Miami.

"We're almost ready," I said. "Only a few more things to do. Those of you who are willing and able to help, please do so, but don't forget to explore this beautiful island and enjoy the sunshine."

Among our paying crew was a delightful couple in their early forties, Sandy and Steve Mayes. Sandy was an attractive woman with blondish hair and a constant smile. She seemed to be looking forward to the adventure. Steve was more seriously inclined but a dependable sort. The couple lived in Maple Ridge, not far from Vancouver. Steve was planning to build his own sailboat, a thirty-six-foot Herreshoff design. He turned out to be a valuable member of our crew.

Then there was Dorothy Sloan, an elderly woman who had been a frequent client of the Vancouver Academy of Sailing and had accompanied us on every weekend trip on the *Anywhere*. She had long white hair that she usually tied up in a bun. She also had a slightly hunched back, but that didn't prevent her from being comfortable aboard a sailing vessel. She and Ray Metcalf had become close friends, and Ray assisted her whenever necessary. Although her capabilities as crew were limited, she was a good companion and was willing to pitch in whenever she was asked.

Barbara Blackman, a pretty girl in her mid-twenties, was also a regular at our sailing school. Barbara had quickly become good friends with Joan, and they shared one of the cabins.

Diane and Gordon Black were another married couple. Diane was a jolly woman with curly, dark hair who soon was deep in conversation with Sandy Mayes. Her husband, Gordon, a skilled carpenter, was a useful addition to our crew.

John Powell, George Howard, Fred Keeting, and Andrew Smith were four businessmen in their fifties who stayed together, forming their own little group. Everyone referred to them as "the four musketeers." I wasn't certain what to think about these guys and hoped they would fit in with the rest of us.

Another group of four consisted of a couple, Richard and Mary Tunstall, with two young sons, Brian and Peter. We all referred to them as "the family." Mary was a quiet and somewhat shy woman, while Richard, a schoolteacher, seemed to be a determined person who knew what he wanted and was very much in control of his family.

Also on board was Danny Tanaka, a cameraman with the CBC, the Canadian Broadcasting Corporation. He said he would be filming the voyage, although I didn't know if he was doing this as a freelancer or on behalf of his employer.

Other crew members included the already infamous Jack Owens, three more married couples, an engaged couple, and a fellow who told us that he was an author. We called him "the writer."

Several of the newcomers were eager to lend a hand with the work still to be carried out. The carpenter, Gordon Black, went to work immediately, finishing off some of the detailing on what we had already done. Sandy Mayes helped Elise with some of her chores, and her husband, Steve, proved to be a skilled person who could tackle any job.

Our cook, Francois, who had also arrived with the newcomers, was busy in the galley preparing a list of the provisions we needed to feed everyone on board. He was in his twenties, a medium-sized fellow with a crewcut, and a bit shy. He moved quietly among the others and spoke softly, engaging in conversation only if he was spoken to. Most often he was seen close to Barbara. He had obviously taken a fancy to her, and I noticed him trying to start a conversation with her, but Barbara didn't seem interested.

I had begun to worry about our cook's culinary skills earlier that day when I asked him to make us a pot of tea. He seemed bewildered by my request. After some delay, I saw him fill a large pot with water and pour the loose tea into the cold water before putting it on the stove. Clearly, he had never made tea before in his life. Elise, who had also witnessed his attempt at making a brew that was bound to be close to poisonous, quickly grabbed the pot from the stove and poured its contents into the sink. She then filled a kettle with water and put it on the stove while explaining the proper procedure to the cook. I hoped that in the mountain resort where he claimed he had worked, making tea was someone else's responsibility.

Later that day, when the provisions started to arrive, my suspicions about the cook were confirmed. Several boxes with unknown contents were carried down the stairs into the galley. Elise called me after she had opened five of the boxes to put the contents into the pantry.

"Look at this," she said. "Five boxes, all full—with ketchup. Bottles and bottles of it!" With a knife she opened another box, also filled with ketchup, then another. More ketchup.

"Holy smokes!" I said. "There must be enough ketchup here to fill a swimming pool. What's going on in this guy's mind?"

Elise picked up the cook's shopping list, which had been returned with the provisions. "Did you see this?" she said, holding it before me.

"No," I said. "It never occurred to me to check it."

I glanced at the sheet of paper: *ketchup, ketchup, ketchup, spaghetti, spaghetti, spaghetti, cheese, spaghetti, ketchup, salt, pepper, macaroni . . .*

"Oh boy, we're in big trouble here. Hopefully we can take

all these things back and get some real food." I thought for a minute. "I guess you'd better make up a new list. I'll ask some of the others to help you."

Disgusted, I went back on deck. How could I have been so naive, so stupid, to believe the cook when he applied for the job? I should have checked his credentials and confirmed his cooking skills. I should have called the ski resort, if indeed he had ever worked there. I was too upset to even speak to our cook as I walked past him. I was ready to have him keelhauled.

From then on, Elise and Joan, helped by other volunteers, did the cooking; the cook was demoted to dishwasher. When we were at sea, however, we discovered that even for dishwashing he was useless. He spent most of his time hanging over the railing, spilling his guts. When he wasn't throwing up, he would sit in a corner on deck, hanging on with all his might while staring vacantly at some distant object.

Chapter Eleven

A few days later the *Raven* was ready for a sea trial, a shakedown cruise. We left the harbour on a blustery day. It was a good chance to put the ship and her crew to the test.

This area of the Bahamas, being close to the Tropic of Cancer, just short of 24 degrees north, is known for its steady northeasterly breeze, usually running about fifteen to twenty-five knots. But in the winter the winds can occasionally be much stronger, especially on the northern edge of the trade winds area. The trade winds belt shifts a bit more to the south in winter.

This was one of those days. We didn't realize how strong the winds were and how much the seas had built up until we saw a passenger liner at anchor just outside the harbour. The big cruise ship was rolling, and spray was blowing over her bow.

The crew took to the halyards, and with many hands at the ropes, the sails were hoisted. With an explosive snap, the wind filled the sails, and after some trimming of the sheets the *Raven* steadied on her course. She dove into the swells and shook her bow as she rose to the next wave. The wind howled through the rigging. Bursts of salty spray flew on deck and over us each time the *Raven* dug into the next wave and then rose to speed into the next one. The new crew members, unsteady on their feet because of this foreign motion, were hanging onto whatever they could grab. Soon many of them were lined up along the railings to obey their protesting stomachs.

Bert had a big smile on his face as he stood at the wheel. He was in his element. I was happy too. The *Raven* was performing well and took the seas effortlessly. There was no question about it; this was a seaworthy vessel. The crew? Well, it would take them some time to get used to it, but many seemed to enjoy the ride. I noticed Steve Mayes busy with Ray Metcalf, coiling up some of the lines.

Steve's wife, Sandy, was holding on to the railing, enjoying the wind and the motion of the bow as it dipped into the twenty-foot troughs of the waves. The glorious spray of salt water shone in the sunlight as it splashed over the decks and everything in its path, drying off when caught by the warm rays of the sun and leaving a powdery white coating on the decks and on everything it had touched. The salt clung to Sandy's face, legs, and arms like white, shining crystals. I noticed her giving Steve a big smile and a thumbs-up.

Three of the four musketeers were also holding up well, as were the two little boys, but their mother was slumped over the railing. She was clearly seasick.

I moved along the deck, inspecting the chain plates of the shrouds and checking the rigging. Everything was good and solid. I went below to check the bilges; some water had entered, but this was normal now that the ship was going through high seas. I turned on one of the bilge pumps. It pumped for a few seconds and then started to make a slurping sound, indicating it had done its job. I went back on deck and into the wheelhouse.

"Everything is as it should be," I reported to Bert.

"Yes, Jan," he said. "She's a great ship, and she handles well. I think we should give the crew some practice. Let's come about and tack."

"Good idea. I'll go on deck and pass the word around." I went to our doctor, Tom, and mate, Ray, and told them what was about to take place. Ray and his helpers would take charge of the mainsail; Tom and his crew would look after the mizzen; and I, with Steve, would look after the headsails. One of the crew was positioned on the deck in front of the wheelhouse. He would shout the orders as instructed by Bert.

"Ready to come about!" he yelled.

The crew stood ready at the sheets.

"Coming about!" he shouted.

Slowly the *Raven* started to turn into the wind. The crew pulled in the sheets as the boat turned, and the wind pressure against the sails slackened. The bow kept turning and slowly moved through the eye of the wind.

"Keep tight on the headsails and ease off on the mizzen" was the next order.

The headsails started to back-wind and helped push the bow around. Then the order came to let go the starboard sheets of the headsails and trim the port sheets, followed by the command to trim all sheets. The manoeuvre was successfully completed. The *Raven* settled on her new course, this time on a starboard tack.

We went through the various manoeuvres many times, and after several hours of going through the motions we headed back to port. While the sails were being lowered and furled away, the engine pushed us along to our destination. The sun was setting, and it was getting dark.

Suddenly, the deck lights we had installed for the arrival of the crew flared up and brightly lit the decks. We hadn't bothered to take them down, since they were not in the way. We thought they might be of use some other time.

When they came on, I happened to be near the bow with a few of the crew. We were getting the mooring lines ready. Tom and his party were amidships, and Ray was at the stern with his helpers, also getting the lines ready. We all stared at the lights.

"What the heck," I said. "How is that possible? Those light fixtures are 220 volts and only work when we are connected to shore power."

Just before we came alongside, the lights went off again.

Immediately after securing the boat, we went to investigate. Was there a connection with the ship's batteries somewhere? Even then, how could that turn on those lights? The maximum voltage we had on board was 24 volts, not enough to illuminate those lights. We traced all the wiring but found no connection. These 220-volt lights were completely isolated from the ship's electrical supply. The only way to turn them on was to plug them into the shore power with an extension cord.

The event was a mystery, and we couldn't find an explanation. It remained a topic of discussion for quite a while. Some people recalled the words of the former crewmen—lights turning on and off, a ghost rambling around the ship—but I shrugged off that possibility. There had to be a logical explanation.

This was when I learned that Chris and Kevin's statements, made when they declined our invitation to sail with us, had apparently leaked to the new arrivals, but so far the crew didn't seem too concerned about the rumours. They treated them as part of the interesting adventure on which we were to embark.

With the sea trial successfully completed, we made some last-minute adjustments and completed the provisioning. We were ready. It was time to leave Nassau and get under way.

Chapter Twelve

On January 17, the *Raven* motored out of the harbour. With all hands on deck, the sails were raised and we were on our way. The ocean had calmed down since our sea trial, and the ship moved much more comfortably through the clear blue waters of the Bahamas.

Bert had laid out a course that would take us through North East Providence Channel, between the islands of Great Abaco and Eleuthera, where there was deep water, and then well into the Atlantic. This first stretch of our route, until we had cleared Great Abaco and Eleuthera, was straight into the wind and was a long haul of constant tacking. Once we were out in the open ocean, we would be able to slowly fall off on a more southerly course to skirt the Bahamas chain, where, unless the wind direction changed, the winds would be in our favour and gradually get us in the area of the steady northeasterly trade winds. We wanted to stay clear of the shallows and reefs near the islands and also make a few stops in the Caribbean, perhaps visiting the Virgin Islands, before heading to Panama.

After darkness had set in, we finally made it through North East Providence Channel and entered the Atlantic. When we were well away from the islands, we plotted a new course. We were still hard on the wind, now on a port tack, but as we progressed the course was again slightly adjusted, which allowed us to slacken off a bit on the sheets. Almost immediately, the *Raven* started to gain speed and her movement became more comfortable. Slowly but surely, the low-lying islands disappeared behind us, their profiles sinking below the distant horizon. Bert took a shot with his sextant, using the stars in the cloudless sky to determine where we were. He went below, did his calculations, and put our position on the chart. Again we altered course, heading a little more southerly.

We were now under full sail. Several members of the crew had gathered at the stern. The moon was round and bright, illuminating the white crests of the waves breaking around us. The onlookers watched in awe as the ocean phosphorescence churned and bubbled happily in the ship's wake, lighting up the dark waters at our stern. Not a word was spoken, nor were any words adequate to describe the splendour of this natural phenomenon. When the spectators reluctantly departed to their bunks, one of them whispered, "It is a privilege just to be here and to have seen that."

Steve and Sandy Mayes, Jack Owens, and the engaged couple, all of whom were on Dr. Tom's watch, and most of the people who had gathered at the stern had already gone below to their quarters when suddenly the lights in the shrouds came on again, lighting up the decks. The entire watch on duty—Ray Metcalf, the writer, the four musketeers, and Dorothy Sloan—witnessed the repeat of this weird occurrence. Bert and I, with Barbara, Gordon Black, and Richard, the father of the two boys, all of us just coming off watch, saw it too. The lights stayed on for about five minutes and then mysteriously extinguished themselves again. None of us could believe what we had just seen.

"It's impossible," said Ray. "Those lights aren't connected to anything. There is definitely no source of electricity to turn on those lights."

"Unless we have a very long extension cord. The shore's a long way behind us," one of the men joked. None of us laughed.

"Twenty nautical miles at least," Bert remarked grumpily.

"I don't know what's going on here," I added, "but I think we'd better take those lights down as soon as we can."

Bert and I talked about the lights some more as we got ready to turn in to our bunks. We could not come up with a logical explanation for their behaviour. We spoke softly, since we didn't want to wake up Tom and Elise, who appeared to be sound asleep. It was well after one o'clock when we both became silent and Bert fell asleep.

I couldn't sleep but continued to wonder about the strange events. First there was the launching of the *Raven* in Nassau at what we thought to be a high tide. She seemed to settle on the ground but then became afloat after the tide went out. In retrospect that was a strange occurrence, although the sand may have shifted. But the yard's manager said he had never seen anything like it before, even with ships larger than the *Raven*. And now those lights—what was going on here? There was no explanation for that. Also, there was Chris and Kevin's talk about a ghost, and their statement that the owners wanted the boat sold because they had witnessed some paranormal events. Was there some truth in that after all? I hadn't seen any ghost, at least not yet; nor had Elise or Tom or Ray or any of the others, as far as I knew.

I finally dozed off and fell into a restless sleep that turned into a dream about some invisible force that stopped me from changing the *Raven's* course. Every time I tried to turn the wheel to stop her from running into a monstrously huge wave—a wave that had two evil eyes and a large mouth—the wheel was turned back, pointing the ship into that gaping big mouth.

The next morning, Ray came into the skipper's cabin. "I've had it with those four musketeers."

"Why, what happened?" Bert asked.

"They drink too much."

"On watch?"

"Yes. I've told them again and again not to bring liquor into the wheelhouse. But they say I'm not their boss, that they paid for the trip and can do as they like."

"No way!" Bert and I said simultaneously.

"We have a strict rule," I added, "and they've been told: no liquor while on watch. Absolutely none!"

"Well, you tell them. And by the way, that other guy? Jack Owens? He's always boozing it up too. You'd better check with Tom. Jack is on his watch, and I bet he also drinks while on watch."

"We obviously have a problem here," I said. "I'll have a talk with them and see if we can sort it out."

I found the culprits and asked them to follow me to the skipper's cabin. "Look," I said when they were seated around me. "Ray told me that you were drinking during the watch. We made this clear at the beginning of the voyage: we can't allow you to drink liquor while on watch! So what's going on?"

One of them shrugged his shoulders. "Ray is exaggerating. We just had a few sips, that's all."

"Yeah," another now joined in. "What's wrong with that? We weren't really drinking, just having the odd sip. Ray makes it sound as if we were stoned out of our minds."

"I don't care," I said. "One sip or two sips—the fact is, you were drinking alcohol, and we can't allow that. So don't blame Ray. He's in charge of your watch. He's responsible and is following our orders. If he tells you not to drink, then don't do it. Those are the rules of the ship, which you were advised of at the beginning of the cruise and to which all of us agreed. Right?"

They nodded their heads reluctantly.

"So, please," I continued. "I don't want to treat you like a bunch of irresponsible teenagers. You are adults and respected business people, so I would very much appreciate your co-operation and not have to go through this type of conversation again."

We shook hands, and they left the skipper's cabin. I hoped this had solved the problem, but as time went on it turned out that my talk had made little impact. Time and time again, problems occurred, especially between the four musketeers and Ray. A few days later they were again caught drinking while on watch. The disgruntled drinkers were promptly discharged and told to vacate the wheelhouse. Not much of a punishment—a good way to get out of standing watch—but what else could we do?

I also checked with Tom regarding Ray's comments about Jack Owens. "Was he drinking while on watch?"

"No," Tom said, pulling the pipe from his mouth. "He's quite a boozer, but, so far, liquor hasn't been a problem while he's on duty. I'll keep a close eye on him, though."

We were still well into the Atlantic and checking the charts for a good location where we could make a landfall and remove the deck lights. We decided to head for San Salvador, a small, low-lying island about halfway down the Bahamas chain (it had the reputation of being the first island in the New World to be discovered by Christopher Columbus), and made the appropriate course adjustment. The wind remained steady from an easterly direction, and the course change allowed us to come on a broader reach, pushing us at greater speed toward our destination.

Most of the crew had started to adjust to the motion of the ship, although the cook and Mary Tunstall, mother of the two boys, were still violently ill and had a permanent spot at the railing. Often they were accompanied by some of the others. Those affected by seasickness were obviously not suited for this type of adventure, but their discomfort made them quick to find fault with other aspects of the voyage. Along with the complaining of the four musketeers, the result was tension on board, which was not eased as the deck lights continued to turn on and off.

On one occasion, all the 24-volt interior lights went off. We searched for an explanation, checking the wiring, the fuses, the battery connections, the switches, but nothing seemed out of order. Then Steve Mayes discovered that the light bulbs were loose in their sockets—every one of them, in every cabin and in the main saloon. How could that be? One bulb, perhaps two, but all of them? We started to wonder if someone aboard was playing tricks. But how could anyone loosen all the light bulbs at once, and how could he or she do that without being noticed? After all, there were plenty of people on board. Were there several culprits? Were they in cahoots with each other? The questions only increased.

The situation became weirder when these interior lights took on a life of their own, not just once but several times. Usually they were loose in their sockets, but sometimes they just switched off for a while and then turned on again.

By now, everybody had heard about the ghost, and some of the crew started to blame it for the unexplainable events. I kept thinking that had to be nonsense—there had to be a logical explanation and soon we'd find out what was causing all these strange problems.

To top it all off, a line had become fouled with the radar scanner. The *Raven* had an exposed scanner, not one contained in a capsule. It was about three feet long and turned constantly when the radar was in operation. The line had wrapped itself around the scanner and jammed it, preventing it from turning.

As we approached San Salvador, I decided this would be a good place to straighten things out and allow everyone to stretch their legs onshore while exploring the historic island.

We went around the eastern side of the island and approached the lee side, where we saw a bay. We lowered and furled the sails, started the engine, and carefully entered a half-moon-shaped bay while taking constant measurements of the depth. This beautiful bay was surrounded by a sandy beach. Some local houses, more like huts, and small boats were scattered on the beach, and a small dock extended about forty feet from the beach. We could not come too close to the shore because the waters were shallow, so we decided to stay a bit farther out and anchor in deeper water.

This was the first time we had used the anchor, and we were having some difficulty with the anchor winch; it would not release the chain. The brake was stuck. It may have seized because of the salty spray we had encountered. With some effort, we managed to loosen it and let out the anchor and chain.

After the anchor was securely set, we launched the dinghy and people started to go ashore. In the meantime, some crew members cleared the line that had fouled the radar scanner, while others removed the lights from the shrouds. Again, as we removed the wiring, we found no connection with the ship's electrical circuit. It was completely separate. There was still no explanation for the strange behaviour of the deck lights. Anyway, now it was all taken apart. The light fixtures and wiring were disconnected, dismantled, removed, and stowed away. They wouldn't cause us any more trouble.

Those who had gone ashore didn't have much to report. The island was small, with low-growing, shrubby vegetation. The few natives who lived there turned out to be mainly fishermen.

The rest of the day, the crew frolicked in the warm water until someone sighted large barracudas circling the ship. Dark shadows on the bottom of the bay turned out to be stingrays, which, although not necessarily dangerous, scared the swimmers and ended the water escapade.

That night we stayed at anchor in the calm bay, a welcome break for those still suffering from seasickness, but the next day we were on our way again. We had decided that since we were back in the island chain, we might as well visit more of the islands. The next destination was Great Inagua, not far from the eastern tip of Cuba and the most southerly island of the Bahamas chain. We set a course to wend our way through the scattered islands, entering via Crooked Island Passage.

When it was time to hoist the sails, something appeared to be wrong with the mainsail. It wouldn't hoist properly. It was stuck.

"What the heck is going on now?" I muttered, climbing on the boom to take a closer look.

Ray, who had followed me, said, "Look, several of these reefing lines are knotted together."

There were two rows of reefing lines in the mainsail. Tying those around the bottom of the sail allowed the sail area to be decreased in strong wind conditions. I looked, and, sure enough, some of the upper reefing lines and some of the lower reefing lines were tied around the boom in a disorderly fashion. That's what had caused the sail's failure to unfurl and prevented us from hoisting it. Another mysterious incident?

I looked around me; several of the crew had gathered to witness this latest glitch. But then we noticed a couple of the women whispering to each other. They looked embarrassed.

"Okay," I said. "What's going on?"

"We forgot to untie the knots," one of them said.

"What do you mean?" I asked. "Did you use the reefing lines for something?"

"Yes," she admitted. "We did some laundry, our undies, and tied them to the reef lines to dry them in the early morning sun."

Gales of laughter greeted this explanation. "Put them in the brig!" one of the crew shouted.

"No, keelhaul them!" shouted another.

The reef lines were untied, and the sail went up without further incident.

Chapter Thirteen

We had a good voyage to Great Inagua, where we arrived early the next morning without mishap—except for another repeat of the loosening of the cabin lights. We entered a narrow inlet into a beautiful bay, well protected from the wind and swells, and came alongside a dock. A few small buildings sat on the beach that surrounded the almost completely enclosed bay. We were welcomed by the friendly inhabitants, who immediately took our crew on shore excursions. They went to Mathew Town, the main village on the island, and explored a salty, marsh-type lake that occupied a large portion of the island. Except for a few hills, the island was flat. Everyone had a good time during our stay, mainly because of the welcome we received from the locals. We enjoyed the island and its friendly people so much that we stayed for two nights.

The evening before our departure, while we were tied up to the dock in the quiet bay, Bert and I were in the engine room doing some service work on the machinery. It wasn't until we had finished with the work and were about to depart that Elise called us, poking her head through the hatch opening to the engine room.

"You'd better come up here," she said, clearly agitated. "We've just witnessed another strange occurrence."

"What's going on now?" I asked.

"Come with me," she said. "I'll show you."

She led us to the main saloon, where Tom, Ray, and several other crew members were gathered. Some sat at the table, while others were standing.

"Look," she said, pointing to the sculpted, eye-patched, pirate head that decorated one of the walls in the saloon. "It suddenly started to move."

"Started to move?" I repeated, walking a little closer to the object. "It's not moving now."

"No, it isn't, but it did. A little while ago."

I looked around to the others, who all nodded their heads.

"Yes," they said, in unison.

One of them explained, "It started to slowly swing and swivel, making it appear as if its one unpatched eye was studying us. Every one of us saw it swing backward and forward. Then it stopped as suddenly as it started. It was creepy."

The others nodded in agreement.

I wondered if this was another indication of the ghost's presence. The others were clearly spooked.

Tom said, "I saw it too, but it must have been caused by some movement of the ship. A movement we weren't aware of."

"But what movement?" one of the other onlookers interjected. "There's no movement. This bay is as calm as a pond in a dense forest. The ship hasn't moved or rolled a fraction of an inch."

Everyone fell silent. Without anyone uttering another word, the crowd dispersed. Each of us had our own thoughts.

The next morning, while we were preparing to leave the island, a truck drove up, loaded with musicians and their instruments. They had come to wish us farewell. As they played, the *Raven*'s crew joined the locals on shore and danced to the band's music.

Jack Owens, a bottle of rum in his hand, climbed on the cab of the truck. He took a swig of the bottle, lost his balance, and fell from the truck. Snap! He appeared to have broken his leg.

With a combined effort, the crew carried Jack on board, where Tom took charge of him. Yes, his leg was broken. Jack lay on deck groaning as Tom went below. He soon reappeared with the necessities to put Jack's leg in a cast. Then Jack was taken below and put in his bunk to rest, bottle of rum still in his hand. Although he had broken his leg, somehow he'd managed to save the bottle.

Eventually we cast off the mooring lines and motored away from the dock. Suddenly it became obvious that there was something wrong with the steering mechanism: when the wheel was turned, the rudder didn't respond. The *Raven* was going in the wrong direction. Desperately, Bert climbed over the stern and wedged his legs against the rudder blade, which was attached to the transom. With amazing strength, fed by adrenaline, he managed to turn the blade in the right direction. Somehow we made it back to the dock, where we were welcomed with loud cheers from the locals.

As soon as we were secure alongside the dock, we started to investigate what had gone wrong with the steering mechanism. It was a simple system: a gear on the steering wheel turned a chain that led from the left and right sides of the wheel down through blocks on each side, then ran along the sides of the wheelhouse and disappeared into a bench, a seat in the aft section of the wheelhouse. Inside the bench, both ends of the chain were connected to a steel tiller, which was attached to the rudder blade.

We determined that the chain must be broken somewhere along its length. We started investigating at the wheel by taking the steering box apart. Everything was okay there. Then to the sides, following the chain; maybe the blocks had torn loose. But there was no problem here either. We followed the chain to where it entered the bench. To get into it and check the connection to the tiller, we had to take the lid off the bench. The lid was screwed down firmly, and it took quite a bit of persuasion to undo the screws.

When we finally removed the cover, what we saw inside was another mystery. The shackles that connected the chain to the tiller were detached from the tiller. But they weren't broken, nor had they come loose from the chain. In fact, they were firmly attached to the chain, with the bolts screwed in place. All of us—Steve, Ray, Bert, Tom, Gordon, and I—stared at the inexplicable. How could this have happened?

"Somebody did this on purpose," said Tom.

"Yes, but who?" Bert replied.

"The writer," said Tom. "Remember? The other day you caught him going through your papers in the skipper's cabin. I bet he's doing all these unexplainable things because he wants a good story."

"That's true," said Bert. "I caught him in my cabin, but how could he have done this?"

"He *couldn't* have done this," I said. "In the first place, there's always someone in the wheelhouse, so he would have been seen. Secondly, how long did it take us to remove this lid?" I looked at Steve, who had taken the screws out.

"Those screws haven't been removed recently," said Steve. "I would say, the way they were embedded, no one has been into that seat for a long time."

"I'll bet it's that bloody ghost," said Ray. "The swinging and the rolling eye of that pirate's head in the saloon was a sign that he was up to another trick."

I didn't know what to say. This had me puzzled. I couldn't think of any logical explanation.

Undoing the bolts of the shackles wasn't easy either. They also appeared not to have been moved for some time. Finally we managed to get everything hooked up again. We turned the wheel several times to test its operation, and when we found no fault, we once again left the dock and departed from Great Inagua, the island with so many friendly people.

Chapter Fourteen

Our stops at San Salvador and Great Inagua had relieved some of the pressure and ill feelings of the crew. Going ashore had provided a break and given them other things to talk about. At the same time, though, we had strayed far from our originally planned route and delayed our voyage to Vancouver. So we decided to abandon the idea of going home via the Virgin Islands. To shorten the trip and make up for lost time, we would make only one more stop, at Haiti. From there we would set a direct course for Cristobal, where we could enter the Panama Canal.

Bert and I were sitting at the desk in the skipper's cabin. In front of us was a sheet of paper. Bert was writing down a list of names—the names of those who didn't fit, who were a constant nuisance and undermined morale. Some of these people were complaining constantly, mostly about the work and the restrictions on their drinking. These complainers should have been on a cruise ship, with all its amenities, rather than a sailing ship where they were expected to pitch in with the work. We had explained this to them well before setting out on the voyage. Perhaps I had been naive to assume that they, like us, were adventurers and that, considering the low fee we had charged, they were all of a spirit that would help the cause of underprivileged kids. I thought I had made clear to them what they could expect once they were on board. Perhaps I hadn't been clear enough. Perhaps I should have been more careful in selecting the crew. Nevertheless, something had to be done about it.

Then there were the people who were still suffering from seasickness—a big problem for some of them—and many of the crew members were uneasy about the strange experiences we had encountered: the lights going on and off, the movement of the pirate's head, and the inexplicable detachment of the steering chain. Virtually everyone was beginning to believe that the *Raven* was possessed by a ghost. It had become the talk of the day and had made even the more co-operative crew uncomfortable.

I pondered the meetings we'd had in Vancouver. John Powell, one of the four musketeers who responded to our ad in the paper, had done some sailing with his daughter and son-in-law, who owned a small sailboat. He had told us that he was considering buying a sailing craft in Japan and sailing it to Vancouver. He said that he wanted to come on the trip for the adventure and to gain experience in sailing at sea. During the trip he suffered from seasickness but often said that he was having a good time regardless.

John had introduced George Howard, the second musketeer, to us. George was about the same age as John, was retired, and had turned out to be an aggressive sort of person. Back in Vancouver, he had stated that he owned a fifty-five-foot powerboat and had made several trips with his vessel up and down the coast. He told us that he was well acquainted with the use of navigational instruments and claimed to be a good navigator. He had offered us his services and skills. He had also said that he was determined to have a good time. When I explained that our journey would not be a luxury cruise, he replied that he was going to make the journey enjoyable and that success depended on the participant's frame of mind. As far as he was concerned, this was exactly the type of thing he wanted to do, so the trip would be enjoyable. During the trip he drank a lot but seemed to be able to carry his liquor. He turned out, however, to be a pushy type who liked to have things done his way. Except for the booze, he performed well on his watches and indicated to us that he was enjoying the trip. He was never seasick.

George had introduced us to the third and fourth musketeers, Fred Keeting and Andrew Smith. Fred, about fifty-five, was a big man with an oversized belly. Later, John and George said that Fred had never wanted to come, that it was not his type of thing, but that he had done so anyway to join his pals. He suffered from a weak heart and drank excessively. He was one of those who was almost constantly seasick, but he was not uncooperative in his duties. He never complained to me, but he was reportedly always complaining to others, mainly about the lack of ice for his drinks. Andrew, like his buddies, drank a lot. He was quiet, except when he was with the other musketeers. He didn't interact much with anyone and was difficult to figure out.

The writer was a strange character. When signing up for the trip, he gave us a deposit of $500 and mentioned that the remaining $500 would be paid later, which it was. He asked both Elise and me to say, if his wife should inquire, that we had charged him only half the cost of passage because he would be such a valuable crew member. He stated that he'd had considerable sailing experience off the coast of South America and had served in the U.S. Coast Guard as a quartermaster. Although he was on the 8-to-12 watch and therefore off duty from 12 to 8, the writer had peculiar sleeping habits. At night he wandered around the ship. Then, armed with eye patches and sleeping pills, he climbed into his bunk in the daytime when others were getting up. The result was that he was constantly complaining about sleeplessness and about the noise made by the rest of us. Our doctor, Tom, advised the writer several times that he should change his sleeping habits to conform with those of other people, but to no avail. He'd rather take pills. The writer performed his duties satisfactorily but was always poking around in areas that were none of his business.

Jack Owens was in his late thirties. During the meeting in Vancouver, unbeknownst to me at the time, he had told Steve Mayes that his interest in the trip mainly involved girls. He had told Elise that he wanted to get away from home and was looking forward to the adventure. Regarding his interest in girls, so far, he had been true to his word: as soon as we arrived in a port, any port, Jack would disappear into a bar in search of booze and girls. He frequently did not return until our departure. And although we regularly did physical exercises on deck and gave lectures about navigation and seamanship, Jack never attended.

While Bert and I were discussing the situation, a small group of the crew had gathered on the foredeck. Nothing stays secret on a ship, and the entire conversation soon found its way to our ears, courtesy of Barbara, one of the reliable members of our crew. Apparently among the gossiping group were the four musketeers, the writer, and Gordon and Diane Black (the carpenter and his wife). Barbara told us that Jack had stood a short distance away from the others, taking the odd gulp from the bottle in his hands, and that the conversation had gone something like this:

"This trip is turning into a horror story," one of the musketeers had said. "They"—he was referring to us—"run this vessel like a navy ship, can't even have a drink. What are they trying to prove? They treat us like we're a bunch of kids. There isn't even a decent icemaker on board. Even off watch, you're lucky to get some ice for your drinks."

Jack, on hearing the complaint, held his bottle up high. "You don't need ice cubes for this," he said after taking a gulp. "It's straight rum. Delicious stuff!"

"Don't let them see you. Otherwise you'll be put into the brig!" the writer answered.

"All you guys can talk about is your drinks and your ice," Diane interrupted. "There are more serious things going on here. This ship is haunted. I heard that on previous voyages, the same things happened. They say there's a ghost on board, and I believe it. It gives me the shivers. The statue that's hanging in the saloon gives me the creeps too. It keeps looking at you with that evil eye."

"I also don't like what's going on here," the writer said. "Too many mishaps. Those lights, the steering, that line fouling the radar scanner. That ghost story is just a cover-up. The reason for all this stuff is that these people are incompetent. They don't know what they are doing."

"I don't agree," Gordon said. "They certainly know what they're doing. They know how to navigate, and they know how to run this ship. They have taken us safely from place to place—not an easy thing to do in these waters. Those other things, the lights—well, I don't know. There certainly are some strange things going on. That rudder situation was certainly a bad thing, but it was resolved."

"Then how do you explain the problems we've been having?" the writer said. "It started with those deck lights flaring up in the middle of the night. They are the ones who installed those lights. They obviously didn't wire them in properly. And why do all the cabin lights keep going on and off? Must also be a problem with the wiring."

"But it wasn't," Gordon answered. "The cause was the light bulbs, which were loose in their sockets."

"All of them loose at once? That happened several times. How is that possible, unless they did it? What other explanation is there?"

"You tell us," one of the musketeers interrupted. "You're the one wandering around the ship all night long. Maybe you're the one who's doing those things."

"Yeah!" Jack laughed. "Maybe you're looking for an interesting story to write about."

"That's ridiculous," the writer responded. "It's them who are doing those things, not me."

"But why would they do that?" Diane now said.

"I don't know. Maybe to cover up their incompetence."

Gordon shook his head. "That doesn't make any sense. They are just as frustrated about those things as we are. And how do you explain the disconnecting of the rudder chain? I was there when they opened up the seat under which the loose connection was found. There's no way anyone could have done that without being noticed. Besides, that seat had not been taken apart for a long time. You should have seen how those screws were embedded in the wood. Also, the dust in that compartment hadn't been disturbed for a long time. No, I'm convinced there is no logical explanation for that."

"It's that ghost, I told you. It's that ghost," Diane said. "Ask the others. Most of them are convinced there's a ghost on board."

"Well," George said, "I don't know about ghosts, but I do know that this trip is not what I expected it to be. This is supposed to be a holiday. I don't want to have to do my own laundry. I want to be able to have a drink when I want one, and I don't want to be told what I can and cannot do."

(Barbara's account of the conversation came as no surprise to us. We had heard this type of discussion before.)

Back in the skipper's cabin, Bert and I were still trying to figure out a solution to the unhappy crew situation.

"I have an idea," I said to Bert. "Maybe we should give the entire crew an option."

"What do you mean, an option?" asked Elise, who, with Tom, had joined us in the cabin.

"It's obvious that many of the crew aren't suitable for this trip. They seem to enjoy the sightseeing on shore but aren't comfortable when we're at sea. We've already made a change by coming here. Why don't we make another change to the itinerary? Instead of going from Haiti to Cristobal, let's offer them a trip to Jamaica. That will be the last stop before Cristobal. When we're in Jamaica, those who don't want to continue can fly back to Vancouver, and we'll pay for their flight. That way, we'll end up with a more compatible crew for the long voyage."

"Can we afford that? To pay for their flight to Vancouver?" Elise asked, frowning.

"We have no choice. We'll have to compensate them for the shorter trip somehow," I answered.

"I think it's a great idea," Tom said. "It should make everyone happy."

"Okay, let's do it," Bert agreed. "Anything to get rid of those assholes. Excuse my language," he added, looking at Elise.

"Let's do it right now!" Elise said. She looked at her watch. "We can do it right after lunch. I'll tell everyone to come on deck at two o'clock."

That afternoon, the breeze was steady and the *Raven* was comfortably carving her way through the relatively calm seas. Occasionally she shook her bow, allowing some fine spray to fly over the decks. Everyone was gathered on deck, soaking up the sun, feeling the salty spray. Some were still a bit greenish due to the motion of the ship. Also the watch, except for Ray, who was at the helm, was present to attend the meeting.

I cleared my throat and began. "It has come to our attention that for some of you, this trip has turned out to be more than you bargained for."

I looked around and noticed that my introduction had drawn their attention.

"That doesn't surprise me," I continued, "because a voyage like this is not to everyone's taste. It all sounds good when you're on land, but now that we are actually doing it, it's a little different from what some of you expected."

Again I studied the reaction and noticed some of the crew

members nodding their heads in agreement. Jack stood by the railing, leaning on his crutch, and seemed to be studying the cast on his leg. The four musketeers were sitting on the edge of a hatch, all of them with serious looks on their faces. The writer, who stood somewhat away from the others, looked anxious to step in with a few words of his own.

I continued. "Some of you are worried about the strange incidents we've had on board and about the suggestion that a ghost is running around in this ship."

Diane Black, who had also been sitting down, stood up and seemed about to speak. I interrupted her and said, "No, please. Let me continue. What I have to say may solve the problems."

She sat down and I continued. "Although the idea of having a ghost on board is doubtful, I have to agree that some unexplainable things have happened. And for some of you, seasickness is another problem that makes this passage difficult to cope with."

I noticed Diane and the mother of the family, both of whom had been having the worst time dealing with the ship's motion, twisting their faces in memory of their illness.

I went on. "So here's an alternative to consider. Instead of going on the long voyage, we can make some changes in our route. To those of you who would rather not stay on board for the voyage to Vancouver, I'm offering a shorter trip. We can go from here—we are already almost a quarter of the way there—to Haiti, which is an interesting island, spend some days there and then go to Jamaica. Those will be relatively short passages, and when we're in Kingston, Jamaica, you can end the trip. We should be in Haiti sometime tomorrow. Then, if we spend a few days there, our arrival date in Kingston can be February

1 or 2, depending on how long we stay in Haiti—that's only four or five days from now. From there, I'll pay for your flight back to Vancouver. Whoever does not want to end the trip in Jamaica can stay on board and continue from Jamaica directly to Cristobal, where we'll enter the Panama Canal and continue on to Vancouver as planned."

Everyone started talking. The proposal was being received with great enthusiasm, and everybody assured me they were happy with this plan. Some came forward to me to confirm that they would stay aboard after we reached Jamaica.

To my surprise, three of the musketeers—George, Andrew, and John—said they were enjoying the trip and wanted to continue. They asked if they could sail as far as Panama and then pay their own fare back home. Although I had hoped they would depart in Jamaica, I had no choice but to agree. They apologized for Fred's behaviour, explaining that this trip hadn't been his idea in the first place. He could not take the seasickness anymore.

As expected, Diane and Gordon Black decided to leave in Port-au-Prince, Haiti. Diane said she felt sorry for her husband, since he was in his element and took great joy in the trip. She, however, was not feeling well.

It was too bad that we would be losing Gordon, because he had been a good member of the crew. As the day went on, others came to tell us that they had also decided to leave the *Raven* in Jamaica. Most of them we were not sorry to lose; once we were in Jamaica, we would encourage a few more to leave. A definite on our list was Jack Owens.

Chapter Fifteen

That night we ran into a strong wind and a lumpy sea. It was the roughest night we had encountered so far. On one occasion the ship took a deep dive, throwing a crew member out of his bunk. We had travelled about ninety nautical miles when we arrived in the Windward Passage, near the northwestern part of Haiti. As we rounded that tip of Haiti, the winds settled down and the seas calmed considerably. More sails were set, and the *Raven* continued toward her destination.

After passing through the Golfe de la Gonâve, we entered the Canal de Saint Marc. When we were closer to the coast, small fishing vessels began to approach. The people in these boats asked us for food and clothing. They were dressed in rags; one small boy was completely naked. This was an easy decision to make: food and clothing, a pair of flared cords, flower-printed undershorts, a golfing hat, and more were handed down from the *Raven*. The wares were eagerly received by the poor souls in their little boats. They were excited with the gifts; one man put on the golfing hat and waved as he departed.

As we came closer to the capital city, Port-au-Prince, we stared at the shoreline, fascinated. On the shore and in the surrounding hills we could see scantily built shacks and huts, mostly covered by palm leaves or straw.

When we entered the harbour area, we hoisted the yellow quarantine flag. This was necessary when entering a foreign port. It meant that we were asking for clearance from the local customs and immigration officials.

A boat approached us, and a harbour pilot climbed aboard. He told us we had to remain at the harbour entrance until customs could come and clear us for entry into the country. For five hours we waited, the pilot aboard all that time, until customs arrived and all the paperwork was completed. Giving the officials cigarettes and soft drinks helped to speed up the process. Finally, with a big hooray, we lowered the quarantine flag and raised the red and black flag of Haiti on the starboard main shroud. We were under way again, this time under the direction of the harbour pilot. Ahead there was a place for us at the main dock, where several freighters were berthed. The harbour pilot guided us in.

"According to the chart, we're heading for a shallow area," Bert commented to the pilot. He had been monitoring our progress carefully.

"No problem," said the pilot. "There's plenty of water for this ship."

He had barely finished speaking when, with a slight shudder, we ran aground. Fortunately we had been moving slowly, and with a burst of reverse from the propeller the *Raven* backed off the shallow spot and moved to deeper water.

Bert promptly pushed the pilot aside and said, "I'll take it from here."

The pilot did not argue. We made it to the berth that was assigned to us without further incident.

As soon as we arrived at the dock, Diane and Gordon Black, armed with their luggage, arrived at the gangway and left the ship.

I thought that perhaps another discussion with the remaining passengers was in order. Again I asked if they wanted to continue, sign off in Jamaica, or leave here in Haiti. To my amazement, three of the musketeers—George, Fred, and John—voted to disembark in Jamaica. Andrew, the fourth musketeer, seemed put out by their decision and said he would stay on board as far as Hawaii, if time allowed. He said he had to be back at work by a certain date. Then the trio took him aside, and Andrew suddenly changed his mind and decided to leave. Three times he changed his vote.

The next day, without any further explanation, the writer and the family—Mom, Pop, and two boys—together with the *four* musketeers, left the ship and boarded a Norwegian liner bound for Jamaica. I can't say that I was disappointed to see the musketeers go. It was the end of our problem drinkers—except for Jack, who had given no indication that he wanted to leave us. Besides being useless because of the cast on his leg, his drinking continued to be a problem. I would have to deal with him later. He definitely had to leave in Jamaica.

I discharged the cook in Haiti and sent him on his way. We

now had a total crew of twenty. Who knew how many of them might be leaving when we reached Jamaica?

Chapter Sixteen

The water in the harbour of Port-au-Prince was filthy and stinking. All kinds of flotsam drifted by and gathered around the pilings of the dock. On shore, the situation wasn't much better. There were ruts and potholes in the roads, open sewers, garbage in the streets. The stench of sewage was ghastly. Yet the streets were crowded with people. Men were drinking from water puddles on the roads, while women bathed their children in dirty water on the sidewalks. In the midst of all this, people were selling their wares, and maimed beggars crawled on all fours. Large, black flies swarmed around the food sold on the streets. The people were astoundingly poor and helpless.

That evening, Tom, Elise, and I went ashore as Bert and Ray stayed on board as watch. After exploring the town a little, the three of us ended up in what we thought was a restaurant.

We came in for a short rest and hoped for something cool to drink. It turned out that the restaurant was actually a bar, with some interesting sidelines. As we studied our surroundings, we noticed Jack Owens stumbling up the stairs, aided by the crutch Tom had made for him on the *Raven*. He was also being aided by an intoxicated woman who was dragging him, arms wrapped around his waist, up the incline.

"Come on, sweetie," the woman cajoled, "I'll take care of you. I have a cozy room just a bit farther up the stairs."

"Did you hear that?" said Elise.

"Isn't that something," said Tom, puffing his pipe. "Even a broken leg in a cast doesn't stop that guy."

"I hope he uses some protection," Elise said. "Otherwise his wife may end up with complications."

"His wife?" said Tom. "I didn't know he was married."

"Apparently he is," I said. "I was told so by one of the crew."

We watched until Jack disappeared from sight as he and his date entered a room at the top of the stairs.

"I've seen enough," Elise said. "Let's get out of here."

We stood up and walked back to the *Raven*, no longer interested in getting that cold drink.

When we arrived, Ray told us that the pirate statue had been acting up again.

"What happened?" I asked.

"Some people came running out of the saloon, claiming that the statue was moving again. One of them said it was scary and thought it was up to something. He said something bad was going to happen."

"Did you see it?" Tom asked.

"No, I wasn't there when it happened. I was on deck when

they came storming out," Ray said. "And I agree with them, that guy has an evil face. It's up to something! Ever since we were in Great Inagua, it's staring at you with that one evil eye no matter where you stand in the saloon."

The previous incident was still fresh in my mind. And yes, Ray was right: the one eye seemed to follow you as soon as you entered the saloon. Just the same, I couldn't help laughing at his reaction.

"Come on, Ray," I chuckled. "It's only a chunk of plaster or moulded clay. Just a decoration. Let's not get carried away with all those fantasies. That following eye must be an optical illusion."

"Maybe, but a lot of strange things have been happening on this ship."

"Are you suggesting the statue is responsible for that?" I asked.

"Well, I don't know," Ray answered, "but I still don't like that thing. And now it's clear that the others are haunted by it too."

"I wouldn't worry about it," I said. "That statue is just a statue, a decoration on the wall."

Ray mumbled something, then shrugged his shoulders and left.

That evening we were all gathered around the large table in the saloon for dinner. Only Jack was missing, as usual. Whenever we were in a harbour tied to a dock, Jack was exploring the local bars.

"I heard the pirate has been active again," I said, raising my voice so that everyone could hear me. My remark was met by silence. The crew just stared at their plates.

A few minutes went by before Barbara broke the silence. "It started its strange movement again. We all saw it." Looking around at the others, she added, "Didn't we?" Everyone nodded in agreement.

This reaction from Barbara—a reliable, logical, no-nonsense person—gave the event some credibility.

"For some reason it was even scarier this time than when it happened before," one of the crew remarked. "It was as if it was trying to say something to us—as if it was trying to scare us out of the saloon."

"Yes," another said. "I had that feeling too. I guess we all did, because we got out of here pretty quickly."

"And how do you feel about it now?" I asked. "You're all back here, and that statue is still hanging on the wall."

As I was speaking, I looked at the pirate's face. To my consternation, it suddenly started to move. The statue, which was attached to the port side of the saloon, slowly started to swing forward, as if crawling along the wall. It stopped for a second, staying at an angled position, and then began to move again, slowly creeping in the opposite direction, as if it was being moved by something. Everyone was standing up and staring at the statue with expressions of horror.

After a few more weird motions, the statue stopped and remained in its original position. Everyone was speechless.

Dorothy covered her face. "I can't watch this any longer," she said with a shaky voice.

It gave me a creepy feeling too, now that I'd seen it myself. As I stared at the evil-faced object, a shiver ran down my back.

After a few moments of contemplation, we all calmed down and the onlookers, including me, sat down at the table again.

This was followed by everyone starting to speak all at once. They became silent again, and I could feel their anxiety rise when I stood up and walked over to the statue. "Oh my gosh" one of them gasped when, with some reservations, I grabbed the culprit and took it off the wall to study it. I wanted to make sure it wasn't attached to something—a piece of thread or thin wire—that allowed someone to move it. But no, there was nothing that would have allowed anyone to manipulate it. I shrugged my shoulders and hung it back on the little hook that was fastened to the wall. The onlookers expelled a sigh of relief.

Barbara broke the silence. As I sat down again, she said, "It's not only that thing." Her head was bowed toward the table, her long, dark hair covering her pretty face. Somewhat embarrassed and almost in a whisper, she continued, "I've never mentioned this to anyone before, but a few nights ago when I went to the bathroom, I went through that corridor." Without looking up, she pointed at the passageway between the forward cabins. "I saw someone come out of one of the cabins. That one there!" She now turned her face toward the cabin. "But it wasn't a real person. He or she, or it, came right out through the wall and then disappeared into thin air."

"I've seen that too!" someone else joined in. "A few days ago I came into the saloon, and someone or something was sitting at the table, but it seemed transparent. I could look right through it. It scared the living daylights out of me."

Several of the others acknowledged similar observations. It became apparent that everyone had kept these sightings to themselves until now, no doubt afraid of being accused of fabricating silly fantasies.

"I haven't seen anything like that," Sandy joined in, "but

I have had the distinct feeling—I don't know exactly how to describe it—but I definitely have had the feeling that there is something else in this ship besides us. Often, especially at night, I've felt this strange emotion, as if someone was standing right beside me. Yet there was no one there."

After listening to these accounts, I looked at Tom. He raised his eyebrows, took his pipe out of his mouth, and put it back in. Bert and Elise looked sombre. Ray looked at me as if to say, I told you so.

"Obviously," I said, "there's more going on than I've been aware of. So many of you, having experienced similar sightings . . . I don't know what to say."

Tom spoke up. "It's beginning to sound more and more like the experiences the previous crew had on this vessel. Some mysterious apparition wandering through the ship, the troubles with the lights—exactly what those two young guys in Nassau described."

That remark caused everyone to go silent again. Each became lost in his or her own thoughts until Sandy spoke up. "But look at it this way: this is all part of the adventure. How many people could say they'd experienced anything like this? It's a once-in-a-lifetime opportunity! We'll talk about it and remember it for ever. It's definitely not a dull, forgetful, ordinary vacation. We've experienced so much already—the islands, the people, this terrific ship on the ocean. How could we ask for a more exciting experience?"

Sandy's optimistic comments drew us all out of our sombre thoughts. Dorothy started to giggle. "Yes, you're right," she laughed. "What's wrong with a ghost? As long as he doesn't bite, let him enjoy the trip too. Maybe we can get him to give us a hand with the chores. Maybe we should look at the positive side. He got rid of those troublemakers. But he won't get rid of us. He's on our side!" Those remarks made everyone laugh.

"We'll just continue on our way," Bert replied. "Ghost or no ghost, he can't stop us from sailing this ship, but next time any one of you sees him, tell him to stay out of my way."

With that said, an optimistic crowd cleared the table and, except for the night watch, departed for their cabins, hoping for a good night's sleep. Bert, Tom, Elise, and I went to the skipper's cabin and talked some more about the ghostly sightings we'd heard about.

"Looks like we're joining the ranks of ghost ships," Bert commented.

"Like the *Flying Dutchman*," I said.

"Or the *Mary Celeste*?" Tom added.

"I've heard about the *Flying Dutchman*," Elise said. "Isn't that the ship that keeps rounding the Cape of Good Hope and, when it's sighted by other ships, brings bad luck?"

"That's the one," Bert replied. "The legend is that the captain was heading into a bad storm and refused to alter course. He said he'd continue even if it meant that he would be sailing into it until eternity. So he was doomed to continue sailing forever. This was in the seventeenth century."

"Yes, I'd heard something like that before, but what's this about the *Mary Celeste*—another ghost ship?"

"It's an interesting story," Tom replied. "Apparently, back in 1872, the *Mary Celeste* was sighted by another ship somewhere in the Atlantic Ocean. She was under sail but had no crew on board."

"No crew?"

"Not a soul on board. Yet the table was set, with food on the plates, and she was under sail, apparently heading for Gibraltar. The captain of the vessel that spotted her put some of his crew on board, and they sailed her to Gibraltar." Tom paused to recollect. "The ship arrived there safely, and since the captain who had found her wanted to claim her as salvage, a court hearing was conducted in Gibraltar. The officials suspected that the salvage crew had murdered the original crew and thrown them overboard. But this was concluded not to be the case. Ever since, there has been a lot of speculation about the disappearance of the original crew. But no solution has ever been found. There is talk about the Bermuda Triangle in connection with this, and the suggestion that there is another similar type of area in the region where the *Mary Celeste* was discovered. In short, lots of speculation, but the fact of her sailing without a crew appears to be true."

"Another theory," said Bert, "is that the reason for her problems was her name change. Originally, she'd been named *Amazon*. Throughout her history she was involved in mishaps—collisions, the deaths of some of her captains—all kinds of things."

"Wow!" I said. "I've heard about the disappearance of her crew, but I didn't know she had a record of other mishaps."

"Well," said Tom, "let's hope that we and the *Raven* don't get ourselves included in that same infamous category."

We switched off the lights, turned in to our bunks, and went to sleep.

The discussion at the dinner table and the departure of the twelve crew members was a great relief for all of us who remained on board. Our spirits were up. In her diary, Sandy Mayes wrote: "We now had a good solid crew aboard who could take life as it came and make the best of it, with a good laugh." I couldn't have summed it up any better. We were now a crew of twenty, and if Jack departed in Jamaica, there would be seventeen crew after Elise and I left the ship in Panama to take care of the business at home—seventeen able crew members, plenty to sail the ship to her destination.

When we'd first arrived in Haiti and were manoeuvring to get the *Raven* alongside the dock, we noticed that the clutch of the propeller shaft was slipping, perhaps caused by the sudden reversal of the propeller when we had to back away from the grounding in the harbour. The ship did not have a gearbox as such. To engage the propeller shaft, the clutch was pressed down via a lever in the wheelhouse. The forward and reverse motion was controlled by a variable-pitch propeller that was operated by turning a wheel, which was also located in the wheelhouse. When we noticed the clutch was failing, I'd gone down to the engine room to increase the pressure on it by sitting on the floor and pressing firmly against the clutch with both legs and feet. It had not been an easy task, but it had brought us safely alongside the dock. Now was the time to correct the problem. We examined the clutch mechanism and noticed wear on one of its components. It would take some machining to make the repairs.

As it turned out, a little way up the dock was a visiting American warship. It would have an engineer among its crew complement and, I hoped, the equipment to re-machine the faulty part. Our crew had already been visiting the ship, and many of its sailors had come to see our vessel. In fact, they offered us so much hospitality that our laundry was being done on their ship and they were giving us hats and T-shirts with the name of the ship embroidered on them. These presents were followed by freshly baked loaves of bread, cookies, and cakes, and a constant flow of ice cubes. Soon, their crew and ours were the best of buddies, frequenting each other's ships constantly. When they heard of our problem with the clutch, a team of engineers promptly arrived on board, took the clutch apart, and totally rebuilt it on the warship, courtesy of the U.S. Navy.

Our crew was getting used to the filth and smells of the city and had begun to tour the countryside. After one of these excursions, when the crew was returning from its trip, Ray, who was sitting on the dock, noticed Dorothy attempting to step back on board. She slipped and fell into the dirty water. Ray jumped up and tried to pull her out of the water by grabbing her outstretched hands, joking, "You'll do anything to get attention, won't you?" That remark made Dorothy laugh too. Giggling, they both struggled, with the result that Ray lost his balance and joined Dorothy in the filthy water. Finally, after much commotion, they were rescued and rinsed off with a hose on the dock before boarding the *Raven*.

While the crew was on shore leave, we did some provisioning. The next day, a long lineup of women, balancing baskets on their heads, swayed onto the docks. The baskets overflowed with coconuts, bananas, pineapples, oranges, grapefruits, and a variety of vegetables. The women lifted the heavy loads from their heads, and the goods were stowed on board by the crew.

"Lots of poor people here in Haiti," Ray said as he observed the basket-carrying women. "It's amazing, though, how happy they seem."

Tom sighed. "We don't know how lucky we are. It's a sad situation."

As the provisions were brought on board, Bert chatted with the captain of a freighter that was also tied to the dock and returned with some interesting information.

"Local knowledge is always the best," he said. "That freighter operates in this area regularly, and it's heading for Jamaica too. Her captain told me that apparently the winds in Canal du Sud—through which we'll be travelling—up to about twenty miles west from Port-au-Prince change direction completely at about noon. In the afternoon they blow toward the west, and in the morning they blow toward the east. That's good news for us, because we can leave in the late afternoon, which will allow us to make a landfall in Jamaica the next morning in daylight. That will put the wind behind us all the way."

Bert showed me the route. I looked at the line he had drawn on the chart.

"Looks pretty good to me," I said. "So, the clutch is fixed, the provisions are stowed away, and, except for Jack, everyone who was a pain in the neck has left. I guess we're ready to go."

"Yes," said Tom. "No more ghostly sightings reported, we have a nice bunch of people on board, and everyone's had a good chance to explore Haiti. It's an interesting place, but I can't wait to get out of here. I'm looking forward to sailing to Jamaica."

Chapter Eighteen

Since our crew complement had been drastically reduced, the remaining crew of twenty had to be reassigned to the different watches. We maintained our system of three watches, each four hours on and eight hours off. So Bert's watch, which included me, was from 8 to 12; Ray's watch was from 12 to 4; and Tom's from 4 to 8. We assigned four crew members to each watch. That left four on standby, including Jack, who couldn't be relied on because of his injured leg, not to mention his drinking.

When the crew members had been advised of their new postings, we were ready to depart. It was almost three o'clock in the afternoon of January 31 when we left Port-au-Prince. After we cleared the harbour, a steady breeze pushed us at about seven knots toward our new destination. At four o'clock, the watch changed. About an hour later we could see Ile de la Gonâve appearing slightly forward to starboard, about thirteen miles away. The coast of the southern finger of Haiti that extends to the west was a couple of miles to port. We were leaving the bay of Port-au-Prince and about to enter the middle of the Canal du Sud. The wind kept blowing steadily, and the seas were relatively calm, though they were building up as we distanced ourselves from the Haitian capital. The crew members who were not on watch were sitting on deck, soaking up the sun, feeling the salty spray, and looking at the wave crests collapsing and sliding under us. They were mesmerized by the steady motion and the sights around them.

As darkness set in, clouds began to appear in the sky. The watch changed again, and soon it was pitch-dark. Bert and I were in the wheelhouse, while one of the crew was at the wheel. The wind had picked up a bit. In the far distance we could see a few faint lights on the two distant coasts, Massif de la Hotte to the left and Ile de la Gonâve to the right. The crew members who were not on duty had turned in.

It was close to the end of our watch when the door of the wheelhouse burst open and Joan Whiteley stumbled in. Her face ashen white, frantic with fear.

"The ghost!" she yelled. "The ghost was in my cabin."

Oh, no. Here we go again, I thought.

"Calm down," I said. "What do you mean, the ghost was in your cabin? Did you see him, her, it?"

"Yes!" she yelled, her voice shaking. "He woke me up. I was sound asleep, and suddenly I woke up and saw this man standing there, right in front of me. It was dark, but I could see him clearly, he was all lit up—illuminated!"

I grabbed her by the shoulder and moved her to the seat in

the wheelhouse. "Calm down," I said. "Take a deep breath and relax."

While Joan shivered in her seat, the next watch started to arrive.

"What's going on?" Ray asked, looking at Joan's dishevelment.

"She saw the ghost," Bert said, raising his eyebrows and throwing his hands in the air with a gesture of disbelief. "He woke her up." With a grin on his face, he added, "That's what she says."

Soon everyone was gathered around Joan, who was sobbing as tears rolled down her cheeks.

"What did he look like? What did he say?" Ray asked.

"He didn't say anything. He just stood there, waving his arms frantically, as if he was mad ... angry," Joan added.

"What did he look like?" Ray asked again.

"He was dressed sort of like a fisherman, with blue, sort of wide, trousers like bloomers, and a blue jacket. He also wore a cap, just like a fisherman."

"Listen, Joan," I said, "you must have had a dream or a nightmare. Probably because of the discussion we had the other day. Now everyone is beginning to see that ghost. You must have dreamed about it in your sleep."

"But—but—but it seemed so real," Joan stuttered, still sobbing.

"Yeah, I understand," I said. "But it was a dream, nevertheless. I'm positive. Here, take this cup of coffee, drink it and relax. When you're ready, one of the crew will walk you back to your cabin." I poured her a cup of coffee from the jar in the wheelhouse, and after she had calmed down a bit and regained her composure, one of the crew took Joan back to her quarters.

"What do you think of that one?" Bert said after Joan had left.

I shrugged my shoulders. "Let's forget it," I said. "She's had a bad dream, that's all."

"Yeah," said one of the crew, "Joan can be a bit emotional."

"True," I admitted, "but on the other hand, I've never seen her act like this before. It must have been a really bad dream."

Suddenly the door opened again. This time it was Barbara, who had been on lookout. "There's a ship behind us," she said. "It's going faster than we are and should be passing us soon."

Bert picked up his binoculars and stepped on deck. "It's the freighter," he said. "The one with the captain who told us about the changes in the wind direction. She's also bound for Jamaica, and following the same course we are."

Before long, the freighter passed by. It was close, within forty feet of us. A light on her bridge blinked and wished us a good trip. Bert passed the watch over to Ray, and both of us went below.

No sooner had we settled into our bunks than we felt a shudder and heard a groaning noise. Then another shudder and more groaning, creaking, and grinding. We had come to a sudden stop. Bert and I jumped out of our bunks and leapt on deck.

The first thing we saw, in the distance, was the stern light of the freighter that had passed us. Otherwise, everything was black. I rubbed my eyes, hoping to be able to see better, but the darkness was all around us. No moon, no stars. Then I saw white crests of waves passing us. The *Raven* heaved slightly, and then shuddered again as some waves passed under us. Reality set in.

We were aground, hard aground! How could this be?

According to the chart, we were in deep water; there were no reefs here.

The wind was still pushing the sails, but the *Raven* wasn't moving. As more crew began to appear on deck, I ran to the bow and saw the white crests of waves breaking on a reef, a reef that was all around us. I ran back amidships and heard Bert giving orders. The sails had to be lowered—no easy task. We had been on a broad reach, almost running before the wind. The sheets of the headsails had to be let go, the main and mizzen sheets pulled in, and the sails pulled down against the pressure of the wind.

I ran to the engine room. Ray had stepped out of the wheelhouse, and as I ran past him I yelled, "I'll start the engine. Put the propeller in reverse as soon as I get it going."

As I entered the engine room, I had a quick look at the bilges below the engine. So far, so good; no water had entered. I released the starting valve, gave a quick turn on the wheel of the compressed air bottle, and injected a burst of air into the cylinders. Immediately the big flywheel started to turn and the engine came to life. I closed the starting valve, hurried up the stairs, and went back on deck.

In the meantime, Ray had put the propeller in reverse and pressed the clutch lever. He increased the throttle, but the ship remained firmly stuck to the bottom.

"We have to put the dinghy into the water!" Bert shouted.

"Right away!" I shouted back.

By this time, most of the crew had awakened. Some were helping furl the sails, while others were wandering about on the decks. A few were standing by the bulwarks, looking over the side at the reef.

"What's happening?" one of them yelled as I ran past.

"We're aground!" I yelled back.

I grabbed two of the crew who were standing by the bulwarks and told them to help me lower the dinghy. I heaved an anchor with chain and line into the small boat as they lowered it. The equipment was heavy, but I managed to accomplish the task in record time.

As soon as the dinghy hit the water, Bert and Tom jumped into it and started the outboard motor. It roared into action and took off. Then it stopped. The motor had hit something and bent the propeller. In the darkness I saw Bert grab an oar and push his way through the water. At a distance of about a hundred feet, Tom and Bert threw the anchor over the side and started to move the dinghy back to the *Raven*. Tom reeled out the chain and line as the dinghy came toward us.

When they were back on board, we attached the anchor line to the *Raven*'s stern, and all of us heaved and pulled while Ray again shifted the engine into reverse. Nothing happened. The *Raven* wouldn't budge; she was firmly aground. We left the anchor line tied to the stern, and Bert started giving instructions to the crew.

"Grab your passports and money," he said. "Put them in a plastic bag and keep them with you. We may have to abandon ship. Also, grab your lifejackets or floater coats and keep them close by your side."

Fortunately, regardless of the panic that had started, everyone listened to and followed Bert's instructions.

"Are we going to sink?" one of the crew asked with a choking voice.

"Not likely," Bert answered. "We're firmly aground. We can't go any deeper. But just to be on the safe side, go and get your stuff and then come back on deck. Don't stay below, because we might start taking on water. Also"—he now looked at Steve—"check all the cabins and make certain no one is still below."

Steve looked around him at the crowd gathered on deck. "Where's Jack?" he yelled. "He must still be asleep in his cabin."

"I'll go and get him," Sandy replied. "You go and check the other cabins."

They both went down the companionway to the inside accommodation of the ship. Another crew member followed to help. When Sandy entered Jack's cabin, she found him still sound asleep. She woke him up, and he immediately panicked. Jumping out of his bunk and throwing all his belongings out of his duffel bag, he explained that he would use it as an airbag if we had to abandon ship. Stumbling up the companionway with the cast on his leg, he dragged the empty duffel bag behind him. Obviously, the liquor was talking.

I headed to the radio in the wheelhouse. Feeling that there was no time to waste, I grabbed the microphone and tuned the radio to the emergency channel, 2182. "Mayday, Mayday, Mayday. This is the sailing vessel *Raven*."

No answer.

I pressed the button and tried again. "Mayday, Mayday, Mayday, this is the sailing vessel *Raven*."

Still no answer.

"Come on!" I yelled at the radio. "You stupid thing! Somebody, answer me!" With my heart pounding, I tried again. "Mayday, Mayday, Mayday. This is the sailing vessel *Raven*."

This time the radio crackled and a voice answered. "This is Coast Guard station San Diego. What is your emergency?"

San Diego? I thought. That's in California! Had our signal somehow jumped all the way to the other side of the American continent?

"Coast Guard San Diego, this is the sailing vessel *Raven*. We are hard aground on a reef approximately twelve miles south off the coast of Ile de la Gonâve, in the Canal du Sud. We have a total crew complement of twenty and require assistance. Over."

"Copy that, stand by."

Bert heard that last message as he entered the wheelhouse. He went to the chart he had spread out on the chart table, checked the radar screen, and took some bearings on lights on the distant shores. With the help of a parallel ruler and a divider, he marked our exact location on the chart, jotted down the coordinates, and took the microphone from my hand.

I looked at the chart. There was no indication of a reef at, or anywhere near, that location.

"I'll take it from here," Bert said. "You'd better go on deck and deal with the crew."

I told him that the station that had responded was located in San Diego.

"San Diego?" Bert looked at me, puzzled. "Are you sure? That doesn't make any sense."

I shrugged my shoulders. "Doesn't make any sense to me either," I answered. "But that's the station that responded. Ask the ghost, maybe he has the answer." I left the wheelhouse and went on deck.

"We've contacted the Coast Guard," I said to put everyone's mind at ease. "Bert is talking to them now."

My message was greeted with great relief. Everyone calmed down.

Steve returned on deck. "I've checked all the cabins, and everyone is accounted for."

"What can we do to help?" one of the others asked.

"Nothing at the moment," I said. "Just gather your things, if you haven't already. Hopefully we can be pulled off this reef."

"Can't the engine pull us off?" someone asked.

"No, we've already tried that. We'll have to wait and see. Bert is still talking to the Coast Guard. Help should be coming soon. Here comes Bert now. Any news, Bert?"

Making sure that everyone was listening, Bert spoke with a calm voice. "They've relayed our problem to San Juan, Puerto Rico. That's the closest U.S. station. I've talked to San Juan, and they are now contacting Haiti. I'll keep you advised as soon as I know more." He turned around and went back to the wheelhouse.

A few minutes later he was back. "Haiti has been contacted," he reported, "but they won't be here until daylight. So we'll be stuck here for a while."

We had few options. Again we tried revving up the engine and pulling on the anchor line, but the *Raven* wouldn't move. As she lay on the reef, she sometimes made a slight roll, and when a wave passed under us we could feel a bump. The aft end would lift to the wave, and then the ship would shudder as her weight was smashed back on the bottom. The forward end appeared to be permanently stuck. No matter how strongly the *Raven* was built, no method of construction would be able to endure that type of punishment for long.

By about five in the morning, we started taking on water. We went to the pumps but couldn't keep up with the flooding. Soon the floorboards in the main saloon and cabins were covered with water. Tom was busy gathering the grapefruits and oranges that were floating around. Fortunately, the freshly baked loaves of bread and pies were still high and dry on the galley counter. We started to take more of our personal gear out of the cabins and put it on deck. Considering our predicament, the entire crew took the nasty situation well. Everyone helped where help was needed. I couldn't have wished for a better bunch of people.

I still had hopes that the *Raven* could be pulled off the reef in one piece. But we needed a tug, or another powerful vessel to do this, and soon. We hoped desperately that such a craft would be coming to our aid. We tried contacting the freighter that had passed us but received no reply. Obviously it was otherwise engaged; the crew was not listening to the radio. And when Bert fired off some flares, there was no response.

Chapter Nineteen

As the hours passed and dawn approached, the prospect of salvaging the *Raven* became more and more faint. There was now a lot of water in her hull. Some of her planks must have been broken or come loose from their fastenings.

We started to salvage some of the gear, detaching the sails from their fastenings and bundling them up, then removing the navigation lights, which were contained in large brass housings, and putting them on deck. Everyone pitched in to dismantle the ship. The activity kept the crew busy and took their minds off our problem.

Bert, Ray, and I struggled with the steering wheel, which was firmly seized onto the shaft. We couldn't get it off. Steve noticed our struggles and approached us.

"Let me give it a try," he said. He grabbed a hammer and

gave the shaft of the steering wheel a strong slap. "Now try it," he said, stepping back.

I grabbed the wheel and, sure enough, it slipped off the shaft easily. Steve obviously knew what he was doing.

As the skies brightened, we could see more of the surrounding area. The reef on which we were stuck was close below us, definitely too shallow for the *Raven,* which needed a depth of twelve feet.

Not too far in the distance, perhaps a mile away, we spotted a tiny, low islet. It was not on the chart either. If it hadn't been for some huts, which at first sight we thought were low-growing shrubs, we would not have noticed the island. The huts seemed to be just above water level.

Soon we saw small, canoe-type boats, paddled by natives, moving toward us. It wasn't long before we were surrounded by them. The natives stayed in their boats, watching us. Some of the crew tried to start a conversation, but these people spoke a language none of us had ever heard before.

Ray and Dorothy decided to visit the small islet and paddled over in the dinghy, but the sight of the elderly Dorothy, with her long white hair hanging loose and her humped back, frightened the natives, causing them to flee and hide. This commotion caused more panic among the many chickens roaming over the islet, which consisted mainly of conch shells. From then on, our crew referred to the islet as Chickenshit Island.

Suddenly we heard a plane overhead. It was a U.S. Navy plane that dipped its wings, turned around, and flew over us again. We waved and yelled. It soon left, but a few hours later it returned. Once more it circled over us and dipped its wings. Then we saw a boat speeding toward us—a small, sedan-type powerboat of about thirty-two feet. It looked like an ordinary private cabin cruiser, but it was operated by the Haitian navy. Help had finally arrived! But there was no chance of getting the *Raven* off the reef with that boat.

It did, however, manage to take eight shipwrecked sailors on board. About six hours later it reappeared and took the rest of the crew, except Bert, Tom, Ray, Elise, and me. We had decided to stay and salvage as much as we could. I instructed Joan to find a small freighter or other suitable vessel that could come and get the salvaged items. I was still hopeful that such a vessel would be able to pull us off the reef as well.

As darkness set in again, the natives in the small boats disappeared. We spent an uncomfortable night sleeping on deck, constantly waking up as the *Raven* moved and pounded on the reef. The next morning, when the sun appeared above the horizon, the natives returned. This time, probably because they had noticed the reduction in our crew, they came closer. Their heads started to appear above the bulwarks. Some climbed on the bowsprit and seemed to be ready to jump on board. We gave them some items—rolls of toilet paper, grapefruits, and oranges that were still floating around in the bilges. They accepted everything eagerly and were friendly, but as time passed they became more aggressive.

The first sign of this change in their attitude and the type of individuals we were dealing with became clear to me when I approached a man and two young boys sitting on our railing. I gave the man three pieces of chocolate, which I had rescued from the ship's stores. Instead of sharing them with the two boys, he put all three pieces into his own mouth and left the boys empty-handed. Shaking my head, I handed a piece of chocolate to each of the boys. As I did so, the man tried to grab the pieces from my hand, but I outmanoeuvred him.

The crowd grew bigger, and some of the natives climbed on deck. We were getting worried—were they going to try to overpower us? Casting about for a solution, I had an idea. On the walls in the saloon were decorative swords and pistols. Perhaps if we put those on deck, where everyone could see them, our visitors would hesitate. Ray and I promptly went below. It was a mess; everything was afloat. The large table had come loose from its fastenings and was adrift, moving with great speed around the saloon whenever the ship rolled and pounded on the reef. With some difficulty, we managed to avoid the floating debris and pulled the swords and pistols off the walls.

Ray spotted the statue of the one-eyed pirate. He ripped it off the wall and screamed, "That bloody thing is the cause of it all!" Coming up on deck, he threw it over the railing as far as he could. "That's the last we'll see of you. You can't do us any more harm!" Ray yelled. The much-hated item plunged into the water, far from the *Raven*.

With much bravura, and making sure the natives were watching, we placed the weapons on a deck hatch within easy reach. It had the intended reaction: the natives withdrew and kept their distance. As soon as the sun went down, they returned to their boats and disappeared. (We later learned that they believed it was bad luck to be out in open water after sunset. Lucky for us!)

During the day, the navy vessel arrived again, and its crew advised us to leave the *Raven*, but we declined. We wanted to salvage as much as we could. We hoped that Joan had by now contacted a larger vessel and that it would soon arrive.

It was on the third day that I realized the *Raven* could no longer be pulled off the reef. I had climbed the mizzen mast to disconnect the radar scanner. When another wave lifted the *Raven*'s stern, and as the ship started to roll, I looked behind me and noticed a slight delay in the movement of the masts. The mizzen mast, which I was on, began leaning to starboard just a moment before the main mast followed its movement. The only explanation for this was that the structural integrity of the *Raven*'s hull had been badly compromised.

This was the last straw. We had lost the battle.

Soon after that discovery, the navy boat returned once more. There was still no sign of a freighter. With the navy boat standing by, I said to Bert and Tom, "I think it would be best if one of us went to Port-au-Prince to try and organize a freighter. Until then, some of us will need to stay here, to protect the salvaged gear from the natives."

"I think it would be best if you went," Bert said. "You're much more likely to succeed in getting a freighter than any one of us."

Tom and Ray nodded in agreement.

"And Ray," Bert said, "why don't you go too? If you guys don't stay away too long, Tom and I will be able to keep the situation under control. Those swords and pistols seem to have done the trick for now. And, of course, Elise, you should go as well."

"I will be back tomorrow," I said. "If I can't get a freighter by then, we'll just have to leave everything, and you guys come back to Port-au-Prince too. It's no longer possible to save the ship, so there's nothing else we can do."

Ray, Elise, and I went aboard the navy craft, and it was with great sorrow in my heart that I left Bert and Tom behind.

After arriving in Port-au-Prince, we were directed to the hotel where the rest of the crew had been settled. As soon as we walked through the doors of this rather fancy place, we were surrounded by the crew, all of them eager to find out what was happening and concerned for our safety.

When I asked Joan about her luck in finding a freighter, she shrugged her shoulders and said she hadn't been able to find anything. It didn't look as if she had given it much of a try; it turned out that she had made friends with some of the more affluent locals and had been busy partying.

Her response made me furious. "What the hell were you thinking?" I snapped. "I was counting on you to get a freighter. Instead, you're busy having a good time while we're stuck on that reef."

"But I *tried*!" she replied, her voice shaking.

"Maybe. But you didn't try hard enough." Not waiting for her response, I turned around and left the hotel.

Frustrated, I returned to the harbour, where I insisted on seeing the commander of the Haitian navy. Without further ado, I was taken to his office, where I explained what I needed. A small freighter was immediately contracted. When I told the commander about the visit from the natives, he frowned.

"Those are dangerous people who are not part of the regular population," he said. "They are outcasts, and live on reefs and atolls. They survive by fishing and stealing. When the equipment is moved from the boat, they will certainly cause trouble. However, I will make certain that will not happen." He picked up the phone and started giving instructions to the person on the other end of the line.

Early the next morning, we boarded the small freighter. Several men from the *Raven*'s crew came with us to lend a helping hand. I soon noticed what the commander meant when he said he'd make certain the natives would not cause us any problems. A number of heavily armed soldiers were accompanying us on the voyage.

It was about nine in the morning when we arrived at the scene. The freighter stayed some 150 feet away from the wreckage, being careful to avoid ending up on the reef beside the *Raven*. The soldiers stood, rifles at the ready, on deck. I hoped it wouldn't come to any shooting, but the natives, seeing the soldiers, stayed well away from us.

The dinghy made many trips. Each time it arrived, the goods were hauled on board and stowed away. It turned out that it wasn't just the natives we had to watch out for but also the freighter crew, because every once in a while some items would disappear. One of those disappearances made Bert angry. He had taken off his captain's hat and put it on the bridge of the freighter, but when he went back to get it, it was gone. He searched and we questioned the crew, but Bert's treasured gold-embroidered cap was never recovered.

As we pulled away from the wreckage, a lump began to form in my throat. With much sadness and despair, I watched the ill-fated *Raven* disappear beyond the horizon. As soon as we had pulled away we saw the natives climb on board, probably to plunder whatever they could use.

While I was staring, Bert told me that the last night had been a bad one. The waves had increased in size, and it had become too dangerous for him and Tom to stay on the *Raven*. They were afraid that the whole ship would come apart. To be on the safe side, they had launched one of the life rafts, tied it to the *Raven*'s hull, and spent the night in the raft, a very uncomfortable experience. They were exhausted.

When I could no longer see the *Raven*, I shook my head and sat down on a bench on the freighter's side deck. I had difficulty stopping tears from welling up in my eyes. Bert was sitting beside me and also having trouble keeping his emotions in check. We sat there silently, thinking about the misfortune that had occurred.

"What I don't understand," I said, breaking the silence, "is the freighter that passed us. It was on exactly the same course we were on."

"Yes," said Bert.

"I saw it after we hit the reef—its stern light straight in front of us. How come it didn't hit that reef?"

"Now that you mention it, I saw it too," Bert said. "I never thought about it, but you're right, it must have gone over the same reef."

"Do you think the freighter had such a shallow draft it didn't hit the bottom?"

"I doubt it," Bert answered. "There was, at most, ten feet of clearance. That freighter was fully loaded and must have had a draft of more than ten feet."

"Well, it would be the only explanation," I said. "It must have had a shallow draft."

"Another thing," Bert interjected. "I double-checked the chart, and there is no indication of any reef there."

"I know," I said. "I checked it too, after you wrote down the coordinates of our location. There's no sign of it."

"And the depth is shown to be well over 2,400 feet," Bert

replied. "Also, that islet with the natives—it should have been on the chart, but it isn't. And it didn't show up on the radar. Mind you, that little pile of rubble was so low and shallow the radar probably couldn't distinguish it from the waves that were breaking over the reef."

"I don't understand any of this," I said, shaking my head.

Bert could only agree. "Neither do I."

The *Raven* glides along under full sail in a gentle breeze. Soon after the ship had left Nassau and was under full sail at night, the mysterious lights were again seen by the crew on deck.

Crew members are hard at work on the foredeck of the *Raven*.

TOP: With the sails furled and the *Raven* at anchor, Captain Bert Mooy and Sandy Mayes confer on deck.

BOTTOM: The *Raven* is under way again, but some seasick passengers are feeling too ill to enjoy the view.

Raven crew members spot a local fishing vessel off the port aft side.

TOP: The *Raven* is seen here stuck on a reef with a lot of water in her hull. The mountainous Ile de la Gonâve is in the background.

BOTTOM: The *Raven* lies helplessly on a reef while her crew lies much the same way, trying to relax while waiting to be rescued.

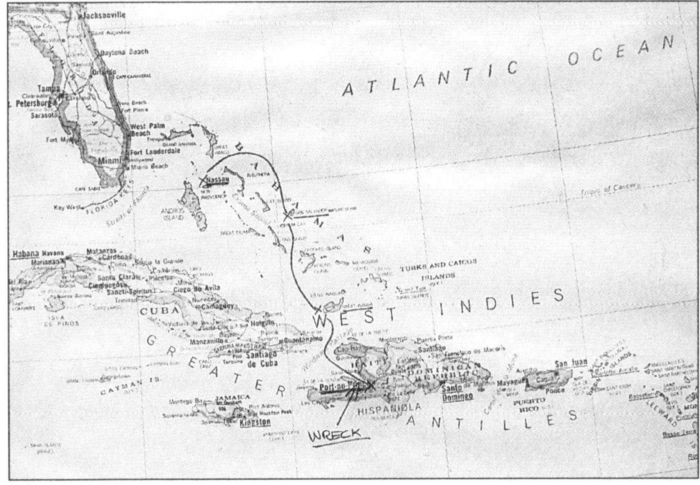

TOP: Crew members pitch in to lower a life raft. At one point, Bert and Tom had to spend a night on one of these when the *Raven* was aground on the reef because the waves had become too high and dangerous.

BOTTOM: Sandy Mayes' map shows the route of the final voyage.

24 TAKEN FROM HAITIAN REEF
City-bound ketch wrecked

Crew safe, but sails Raven nevermore

Shipwrecked 'SV Raven' Mysterious Story Told

Raven doomed by an evil eye?

Reef scuttles holiday plans

JUDGE RULES UNDERWRITERS MUST PAY FOR LOST KETCH

Seen here are some of the headlines from various newspaper articles about the wreck of the *Raven*.

Joan Whiteley with blessed plaque from Raven.

THE PROVINCE, Thursday, February 10, 1972

Dead builder 'walked' doomed Raven's decks

by Roger Marshall

A Vancouver girl who claimed she saw a ghost aboard the jinxed yacht Raven before it was wrecked on a Caribbean reef, identified her spectre Wednesday.

(continued . . .)

This *Province* article, for which Joan Whiteley was interviewed, appeared in February 1972 and contains at least two factual errors: the ghost seen on the *Raven* was that of the original owner, not the builder. Also, Joan was confronted by the ghost about twenty minutes before hitting the reef, not four hours, as reported. The boat's first owner met with a grisly death.

Joan Whiteley, 24, said she believes it was the ghost of the Raven's builder, who was crushed to death between the 110-foot ketch and a dock.

The ketch carrying 20 Canadians was wrecked on a reef near Haiti last month.

"The Raven was being built in 1921 in Denmark under the name Daneborg," Miss Whiteley said. "The builder fell from the dock but nobody knows why the accident happened—or even if it was an accident at all."

It was only twenty minutes before the Raven hit the uncharted reef off Haiti that Miss Whiteley said she saw the builder's ghost.

"I was in my cabin trying to get some sleep before a 4 a.m. watch. Suddenly I felt a creepy feeling and when I looked up there was a man in blue standing there."

Miss Whiteley said the man appeared to be middle-aged and was dressed in Danish clothing of the 1920s.

"He appeared to be ordering a crew about and waving his arms in the air."

The ghost then left, she said, and twenty minutes later she was awakened by the Raven hitting the reef.

After the confusion of the wreck Miss Whiteley was sitting in the wheelhouse of the Raven with Elise de Groot, wife of the owner.

"We were firmly stuck on the reef and in no danger of sinking. Suddenly I felt this clammy creepy feeling again."

"Tears started to come from my eyes and I felt the ghost leave the ship."

Miss Whiteley had flown to Nassau with Jan de Groot, head of the Vancouver Sailing Academy to bring the Raven to Vancouver.

To finance the trip de Groot had offered a sailing vacation

to Vancouver sailing students for $1,000 including air fare to Nassau.

But when de Groot, his wife, and Miss Whiteley arrived in Nassau, the U.S. crewmen who sailed the Raven from Denmark had a strange tale to tell.

"We asked them to sign on with us to Vancouver. But they refused because they said she was a jinxed ship and had seen the ghost themselves."

The Raven was almost sunk in a storm in the Bay of Biscay en route to Nassau.

The crewmen told of footsteps in the night and a series of unexplained accidents during their marathon voyage to the Caribbean.

The Raven sailed from Nassau with 33 aboard. Even then de Groot was aware of two sea superstitions that the Raven had broken.

"It is bad luck to change the name of a ship," said Miss Whiteley. "And it is also bad luck to name a ship after a bird."

When Raven left Haiti last month she was to have counteracted the superstitions by changing her name back to Daneborg.

But there was a snag. Her captain was Dutch-born Bert Mooy and the vessel had to be registered in a Dutch port to make the renaming valid.

The Raven was to head for Jamaica and then to the port of Curacao in the Dutch Antilles. She never reached the Antilles.

"I believe the Raven was jinxed when the builder was killed," Miss Whiteley said.

Chapter Twenty

When the freighter arrived at the dock, we loaded the gear into a truck. I had made arrangements with a shipping agent for the goods to be put into a container and shipped to Vancouver. The shipping agent had arranged for the truck and promised to take care of the goods from there.

Elise and I went to the hotel, had a shower, and tried to relax. But many details were still to be taken care of. I had to make arrangements for the crew to return to Vancouver. This had to be done as soon as possible, because the hotel bills were adding up rapidly. I knew I'd have to deal with the reality of hotel bills and plane tickets later. We also had visits from local dignitaries and members of the U.S. consulate, who told us an interesting story.

Apparently the U.S. warship that had left the day before we

did was at the northern end of Haiti, in international waters, when we hit the reef. The U.S. Coast Guard in Puerto Rico asked the warship to come to our aid, but the Haitian government refused to let it into Haitian waters. This became a minor international incident because the U.S. Navy announced that unless the Haitian navy came to our rescue immediately, its warship would enter Haitian waters whether they liked it or not. The Haitian navy reconsidered and then agreed to send a vessel. To make certain this was being done, the U.S. authorities sent the plane that we had seen circling over us to monitor the situation and ensure the Haitian navy was coming as it had promised. In the meantime, the U.S. warship had been standing by in case the Haitians did not fulfill their promise.

While we were in Haiti, we were treated well. A government official regularly asked if he could be of any assistance. We also had frequent visits from newspaper reporters and received telephone calls from reporters in distant countries. Their newspapers spread the story of our misadventure throughout the world.

After a few more days of paying bills and giving our best wishes to the rest of the crew, Bert, Tom, Ray, Elise, and I thanked the officials, said goodbye to Haiti, and boarded a plane back to Vancouver.

Upon our arrival, we discovered that our mailbox was filled with letters about related stories. One of them contained an article that had appeared in the Dutch boating magazine, the *Waterkampioen*.

This article is a remarkable story about something that had happened to the *Raven* before I became her owner. With the permission of the *Waterkampioen*; the author, Cees van Staal;

and the *Raven*'s skipper, Captain Jaap Stengs, I have translated
the article from Dutch into English.

The Miracle of the Raven

by Cees van Staal

Let me first tell you who I am. My name is Jaap Stengs.
I have been at sea as a professional captain for about
eleven years, delivering large and small yachts to wherever their owners want them to be taken.

I will now tell you the story of the *Raven*, a ketch of
99 gross registered tons built by Randers in Denmark
in 1920. She was built of four-inch oak planking over
an inner skin of three inches. One registered ton is 100
cubic feet of space, which is equal to 2.83 cubic metres,
and that multiplied by 99 delivers 280.17 cubic metres
of total interior space. One cubic metre is capable of
holding one metric ton in weight of water. Her load-
carrying capacity was 180 metric tons of dead weight.
The tug *Torres*, which towed us into Musel after the
storm, pumped 200 tons of water out of the *Raven*.
With that much water inside her, she should have sunk
and certainly should not have been able to sail without
capsizing. But she stayed upright and afloat, and that is
the miracle of the *Raven*.

I arrived on the *Raven* because the owner, Tay
Moltsberger, decided he needed a captain familiar with
the route to take the ship across the Atlantic. Tay had
organized a number of individuals who had pooled their
money to buy the *Raven* as a vacation ship for exploring the Caribbean. With a crew of three women, Tay

had started his voyage, but when bad weather damaged *Raven*'s rigging, they entered the Dutch harbour IJmuiden for repairs shortly before Christmas. He moored the ship in Amsterdam.

The crew of three women was now joined by the actress Jean Aubrey and three men. Linda, Tay's wife, had completed a course in coastal and celestial navigation. Susy Farmer, girlfriend of Mike Seymour-Sloane, took care of the domestic chores on board. Mike and Micky Lee had seagoing experience. Noël Hamilton walked the deck of a ship for the first time in her life; she was on board to write a book.

Before I accepted the job, Tay and I inspected the ship. He told me that the rigging had been renewed, the hull seams had been recaulked, and new zinc anodes had been installed to protect against electrolysis. A three-cylinder B and W Alpha diesel engine was located in the engine room. At 350 rpm, this engine delivered 150 HP to the two-bladed variable-pitch propeller. The *Raven* was outfitted as a gaff-rigged ketch with approximately 232 square metres of sail area. The electronic equipment couldn't be better: radar, recording depth sounder, autopilot, a Sailor 66T receiver with direction finder, and a Sailor 76D radio transmitter of 30 to 50 watts.

Bad repair

An inspection like this is of course limited, since the inner hull sheathing restricts access to the inside of the actual hull of the ship. Therefore, nobody knew that an old repair of a strake near the keel had been carried out so poorly that it later almost caused our sinking in the Bay of Biscay. In fact, the chief shipwright of the shipyard in the north Spanish harbour of Gijon determined that a side of the repaired strake had not been properly shaved. Because this strake did not meet with the adjoining strake as it should, the caulking material that had been put into the V joint was pushed inwards when the ship encountered heavy movement during stormy weather.

The *Raven* was to sail to Corpus Christi, Texas. The best route for this trip was via the Canary Islands and Antigua. That way, the current and the trade winds would be with us, pushing us toward our destination. January is the most hurricane-free month in the Atlantic Ocean, and we planned to reach our destination in mid-March.

We left Amsterdam the day before New Year's Eve and crossed over to Ramsgate, in England, to have our autopilot inspected by the factory, which was located near this harbour. We stayed alongside there for a while, because the southwesterly grew to a heavy force 7 and kept holding its strength. Around January 10, the weather improved, and with a favourable wind we made it directly to Portsmouth. On January 14, we left from there at 14:04 hours on a west-by-south course. For the first few days the weather remained good, which gave me the opportunity to concentrate on familiarizing the crew with their duties on board.

We made our way through the English Channel and then into the Bay of Biscay. The next morning,

during the day watch, crew member Morris Parker, who
I haven't mentioned yet, fell from the companionway
stairs in the saloon. That was not mentioned in the
logbook because, after a careful examination, I found no
indication of serious bodily injury. It's better to forget
my diagnosis, because the fall had broken a bone in his
leg. That became clear later, when he was examined by
a doctor in Spain. I hereby take my hat off to Morris,
who all those days during the storm, and regardless of
his great pain, faithfully performed all his duties as a
seaman.

I planned to travel straight to Las Palmas, Spain,
keeping Cape Finisterre close to the east of us.

Tear in mainsail

Monday, January 28. Northwest of Finisterre, we came
into an area with strong winds. As we were reefing the
mainsail, the aft section tore apart. We were able to
make a reasonable repair, but since we were short of
certain materials, and the sail had been badly damaged,
we were unable to repair it sufficiently to allow us to reef
it properly. We therefore continued only under mizzen
and headsails. I informed Tay that I wanted to enter
El Ferrol or La Coruña to have the sail professionally
repaired.

The next day the wind came from the southwest
at force 8 to 9 Beaufort, so I changed my plans. Under
those circumstances, La Coruña and El Ferrol are situated on a lee shore. The coast there is steep and rocky,
with a fast-rising bottom, which, during bad weather,

causes rough seas and heavy swells. This presents a life-threatening situation to any ship trying to enter these ports—all good reasons to change course to a westerly direction in order to obtain as much sea room as possible.

Westerly course

In the evening, at 23:20 hours, we spotted Cape Prior on our radar at a distance of 16.8 miles. A little later, between the fast-moving dark clouds and rain showers, we could see the light of the cape. I went to my bunk to sleep after giving the crew directions to keep the ship as close to the wind as possible, and to awaken me if anything untoward happened or the wind direction changed. I had a premonition that more was in store for us and decided that, in the meantime, I'd better get as much rest as possible. The next morning I was awakened early with a report that the wind had indeed backed to WSW.

In the wheelhouse I checked the course and dead-reckoning position and gave the order to come about. At 06:40 hours on January 20, I turned on the receiver, which was already tuned to 200 kHz, to listen to the BBC shipping forecast: Biscay and Finisterre, north-westerly, force 8 to 10. I therefore did not doubt for one moment the correctness of my decision to stay on a westerly course as long as possible, so that later, when the northwesterly returned, we would be in a position to round or double Cape Vilano and exit the Bay of Biscay.

During the night we had set the mainsail again

in order to gain speed, but now the wind started to increase, this time to force 9. We went with three hands forward to lower and stow the mainsail. Twenty minutes later, the ship was sailing again under jib and mizzen. We came about again, and our course became 280 degrees.

From below I was advised that after pumping the last time, there was a lot more water in the bilges than normal. An estimate of the amount of incoming water in one hour worried me.

That worry didn't leave me when there was a new problem on deck that had to be solved. It was about eleven o'clock when the wind suddenly shifted to south by west, becoming stronger. Over the old westerly swell of the sea came a new one from the south, causing short, lumpy seas. The ship worked into this with so much might that the mizzen mast, with sail bent, swayed like a tree in the wind. I decided to move the ship before the wind at a broad reach—at an angle of 160 degrees from the wind.

Hurricane

And then the hurricane started. The wind shifted a little more to the south and started to howl. Someone pulled my sleeve and shouted in my ear that the ship was taking on a lot of water. I had no time to react to this; the mizzen had to come down. There were no men available—two were at the wheel, two were in the engine room trying to get the pumps going, and one was on deck operating the manual deck pump. The mizzen was sheeted out so far that the gaff and the upper part of the sail were pushing against the shrouds. I loosened the peak halyard, but nothing happened. The gaff stayed pressed against the shrouds. With a Handy Billy [a block and tackle], I climbed along the sail hoops up into the mast. I tied the line to the claw of the gaff, let myself down, started to pull, and managed to get it a few centimetres above the boom. Furling the sail was impossible. I put my knife into the lashings that fastened the sail to the gaff and cut them, then tied the loose pieces of sail that were left to the mast.

My watch showed that I had been busy with "Operation Mizzen" for one hour. Now I was worried about the poor visibility. We were in the middle of the shipping route, and foam from spray meant our visibility couldn't be more than a couple of hundred metres. The radar had packed it in because of the shaking of the mizzen mast, to which the radar scanner was attached.

Every now and then the motor pump failed. I could hear that when the motor stopped running. I yelled at the crew below, wanting to know what was happening. Mike came up from below and silently showed me his opened right hand. Among all kinds of junk were large pieces of caulking material, which indicated that a lot of caulking was being pushed through the caulking seams and ending up between the outer and inner hull. That's why the ship was leaking so badly, and that's why the pumps kept failing: the stuff was plugging their intakes. In the meantime, the crew had formed a chain gang and was bailing water with buckets, hauling them ten feet up.

A little while later, the motor pump started again. The crew down below was working like horses. I was told that they were getting the freshwater pump, the waste pump, and the oil pump ready to help pump the bilges.

At 16:40 hours the storm eased off. In books it says, "It stopped as suddenly as it started"—but a substantial force 8 wind remained from the west, and the seas were enormous.

Meal time

I called Jean Aubrey and told her to stop whatever she was doing and start preparing a nourishing meal. To eat while at sea is as important as breathing: one needs lots of food to replenish the energy used. Also, calmly sitting at a table with hot food keeps up the spirits and gives one the feeling that everything is under control.

While I sat at the table, I was constantly thinking about the pumps. If they eventually failed, we would be in big trouble. I had to lower the risk. After the meal—which, incidentally, had been very well prepared—I went to the radio, tuned it to the emergency channel 2182, and started a pan call. "Pan, pan, pan, to all ships, Charley, Quebec, pan, pan, pan, Delta, Echo, Raven," which means "To all ships: I have an urgent message about the safety of my ship." Finally I made contact with Radio La Coruña, the operator of which, like the operators of all Spanish and Portuguese stations, was unable to speak or understand English. With my limited knowledge of the Spanish language, I managed to explain what was happening to us.

The operator answered that no one—no lifeboat, Coast Guard vessel, or other vessel—was available to help us. "Try to get hold of a fishing boat," the operator said. "Then they can bring you a pump."

The BBC weather channel for shipping gave a forecast at 18:00 hours of northwesterly winds ranging from force 8 to 10 for our area. So it was not possible to head for La Coruña. I decided to heave the ship to the wind. The only harbours from which I had a chance of receiving help were located on the northern shoreline. The others were too far to the south, past Finisterre, or all the way to the east, inside the Bay of Biscay.

All of a sudden, a loud Dutch voice boomed out of the loudspeaker. "Hello, *Raven*. This is the *Smiths Lloyd 18*. I have heard of your condition, am sixty miles south of Cape Villano. I am coming for you! Tomorrow morning I'll come around the corner and then, instead of going to Quessant, I'll change course to your position. Over."

We couldn't stay hove to, because we were drifting toward the coast. I ordered the helmsman to steer 30 degrees and to adjust the sheets of the jib accordingly. Soon we were once more moving at reasonable speed, heading north northeast.

Spanish north coast

I decided to try and enter one of the bays on the north coast of Spain to the east of Punta de la Estaca. I knew Ria del Barquero and Ria de Vivero from previous voyages; in addition, we had charts on board of those locations.

I tried to take radio bearings, but the frequencies I needed were distorted by heavy interference. Only a bearing on Villano was operational. I didn't trust the console counts on Lugo. The high mountains create a lot of land interference, and as a result the dots and dashes can deviate by several degrees. Everyone had been instructed to look for light beacons on shore, but they remained invisible. So I had to assume we were outside the light circles I had drawn on the chart. Still, there was a chance that we were closer to the coast than we realized. The sailing directions stated that the lighthouses on the high rocky coast might be obscured by clouds in this sort of weather.

I radioed Captain Sybrant Steenbeek of the *Smiths Lloyd 18* and told him I would be off the air for about four hours to get some sleep.

He answered, "Right you are. Over and out."

At 07:00 hours on January 21, I woke up because I felt someone shaking me. I had come out of a deep sleep. When I arrived on deck, the wind was still from the west. Tay had listened to the weather forecast and reported a warning for another storm from the northwest. Under these circumstances, the ship couldn't come closer to the wind than 120 degrees. I found it sensible to keep heading on a northerly course; we could change course to 45 degrees later. That way, I would accomplish an approximation between moving up higher and keeping some speed.

At 07:45 hours, I took another bearing on Lugo. The result matched closely with my estimated position. There was no sun, which was unfortunate, because the position line would have provided additional information regarding our location.

I called Steenbeek and explained how I had calculated my estimated position. Together we came to the conclusion that my calculation was probably correct.

At 09:00 hours, the *Smiths Lloyd 18* radioed that it had reached a position twenty miles north of Cape Villano. At 08:00 hours we had changed our course to 90 degrees because, according to our estimated position, we were now twenty-six miles north of the latitude of Punta de la Estaca. Captain Steenbeek told me he could not detect us.

We were now running straight before the wind. There was still so much wind that every once in a while the log line blew on deck and became twisted around the head of the rudder or the davits. Meanwhile, our radar was made functional again. There was no sign of the *Smiths Lloyd 18*, nor could we see the coast. The range of the radar was twenty miles; at least this indicated that we had sea room.

At 12:45 hours, I changed our course to 148 degrees. According to my estimation, this course should take us into Ria de Vivera. One of the women came to tell me that the water inside the ship was coming in as fast as they could pump it out. I realized that if the main pump decided to quit, we would be in great danger.

At 15:40 hours, we were passing the 215 line of the

continental plateau. I now could check how high the seas were by following the recording depth sounder. My estimate appeared to be correct; the ship moved up and down at an average of twelve metres (almost forty feet) in relation to the sea bottom.

I needed a position that was as accurate as possible. There was no sun, so the only alternative was to calculate a good position via the radio direction finder. I had the generator stopped to limit interference and quickly took six fixes on Lugo, of which I received 198, 196, 191, 197, 195 and 192. I calculated the average and put it at 195 degrees. At the same time, the depth sounder recorded a depth of 182 metres. I also tried to get a fix on Cape de Peñas, but there was no response on that frequency. (I had no way of knowing that this station had stopped broadcasting twenty-six hours earlier because the storm had broken its antenna.)

Chance missed

It turned out that we were twenty miles east of our estimated position, which meant we missed our chance to enter one of those easy bays. Hanging over the chart table, I studied the detailed charts of the harbours of Cape de Peñas. As I was doing this, a few other things went through my mind; the water coming into the ship would definitely sink us if the main pump failed. Also, in a few hours it would be dark, and entering one of those small harbours in a condition of rough seas and swells close to the coast would not be an easy task. I knew from experience that the lighthouses in the small

harbours of these countries were often extinguished or
not operational. Besides, for manoeuvrability I had to
rely on the jib and an engine that was becoming unreli-
able because of water in the engine room. The mizzen
I had cut to pieces during the storm, and the mainsail
could only be used without a reef.

Onward to Musel

I decided to stay at sea and continue to sail to Musel.
That harbour was situated in the shelter of the northwest protecting land and had a spacious and easy
approach. Musel was also a busy port and had a pilot
service and tugs available.

I doubted that Steenbeek would be able to find us.
Something must have gone wrong with our communication about our location. That's why I hoped that, once
we had rounded Cape de Peñas, we would be able to
make contact with Gijon radio, through which we could
arrange for a tugboat with pumps.

Again I called the *Smiths Lloyd 18*. This time, in
reply, I received a new answer: "Echo, Delta, Foxtrot,
Zulu, *Virgin de Los Reyes*, position 43.43 North, 06.25
West. I am steaming in a westerly direction. I am coming to you."

The captain of the *Virgin de Los Reyes* sounded like
a determined person, and I decided to thank Captain
Steenbeek for his efforts. If he continued searching for
us any longer, he would run out of fuel. The voice, which
had become so familiar and trustworthy to me during
the last twenty hours, had a compassionate sound when

it came through the loudspeaker: "Good luck, Stengs, over and out."

By 20:00 hours, I was tired and decided to get a few hours of sleep. The wind had turned to due west. I gave orders to steer course 75 degrees for twenty-five miles, and then to jibe and set course for Gijon. I ordered Tay to wake me up the next morning at 04:00 hours.

Sinking

At 23:20 hours, before Tay's hand could touch me, I woke up. Tay stood next to my berth. He didn't have to tell me what was happening. The sound of the motor pump was gone. Although I could hear the other pumps operating with intermittent hiatuses of failure, it was as if everything had gone very quiet on board.

Tay looked at me and nodded. "It has definitely reached its end. The pump housing and the pipes and hoses are full of caulking and junk from the bilges. It's no longer possible to repair!"

I stayed silent for a minute. We were now a sinking ship. I fought a feeling of panic.

I had the crew change tacks and I went to the chart table and made my guess; we were about thirty-five miles to the northwest of Cape de Peñas. I waited until precisely 24:00 hours. This was the moment for Mayday. It would be the first time in my life that I would pronounce that word on the radio.

Once more I checked the antenna's power. I then picked up the microphone in my right hand, pushed the transmitting button, and heard myself say, "Mayday,

Mayday, Mayday, Delta, Echo, Raven, Raven, Raven." I
waited for a moment and then, "Mayday, Raven, position thirty-five miles, repeat, terra three penta, thirty-five
miles northwest Cape de Peñas. I am sinking, over."

I released the transmitting button, heard a "send"
sound in the speaker, a crackle, and then a voice with
a strong Spanish accent, "Raven, Raven, Raven, this is
Butatres, Butatres, Butatres, received Mayday, position
43.48N, 04.52W, Captain Francisco Grande Alvarez gives
order to steam full speed. In this sea eleven knots, over."

The captain repeated the message in Spanish. I made
a speedy calculation. At a distance of sixty-three miles, it
would take him six hours to reach us.

At 03:00 hours on January 22, the water inside the
ship was reaching well above the turn of the bilges. I
realized that the free-liquid surface area, covering the
full length and breadth of the ship, was becoming so
large that it would affect our stability. There was now
a chance the *Raven* would capsize. The moment of
sinking can be predicted, but the moment of capsizing
cannot.

I thought about our predicament for a minute and
then gave the crew orders to exchange their boots for
running shoes; put on sweaters and life jackets; place
their passports, other important papers, and money in
their pockets; and carry as much chocolate as possible.
With two men I went forward to lower the jib and the
staysail to lessen the heeling pressure on the ship, and I
changed the course to running directly before the wind.

I called the *Butatres* and informed her mate, Enrique

Caño, that we might capsize any minute and that we would leave the ship if the situation became too dangerous. I advised him that this might happen so suddenly that we would not be able to communicate this by radio.

The water had risen more than a metre above the cabin soles. The stability should have become very tenuous, but something strange was going on in the ship. With a stopwatch I checked the time it took the ship to recover to an upright position after heeling to port, then starboard, and back to port and upright again (this is called the rolling period). Four seconds. That was strange. If the ship's stability had been compromised, the recovery period should have been much greater. I waited twenty minutes and repeated the observation. Again, four seconds. Twenty minutes later I checked it once more. Still four seconds! I was now convinced that the time of sinking or capsizing lay well in the future. I ordered the crew to carry on with the hand pumps as I called the *Butatres* and told them that we would not be leaving the *Raven* for some time yet.

The speed at which water was entering the ship had started to slow down, probably because there was so much water inside the ship already that the difference in pressure between inside and outside had decreased. I thought about this and concluded that it made sense to try and get a tow line over to the *Butatres*.

I called them again on the radio and asked if they would be willing to tow us into the harbour of Musel if we were still afloat. They listened to my reasoning and agreed to the proposal.

Suddenly from the deck someone yelled, "Ship in sight!"

I leaped onto the deck and saw the lights of a fishing vessel. With the Aldis lamp I signalled SOS; no answer! I asked for two red parachute flares and fired them off. Not a sign of life. *Why don't those damn guys respond?* I thought. The ship passed us at close quarters. The lights were on in the wheelhouse, but there was no sign of a soul on board. It spooked us. It looked like a ghost ship.

The *Butatres* gave me their position at regular intervals. They were approaching quickly; faster than eleven knots. The captain was pushing his ship against all odds in those rough seas.

At 05:00 hours, I asked Jean Aubrey to start shining the searchlight at regular intervals against the low clouds in the direction from which the *Butatres* would be arriving. We were all standing on deck, staring into the dark night. Then one of the crew shouted, "Lights, lights, lights!" and we all cheered. The ship came closer: I noticed it was a gas tanker.

I ran to the radio, pushed the speaking button, and noticed that there was no antenna signal. At the last minute, the radio had quit operating. I ran back on deck, grabbed the Aldis lamp, and signalled our ship's name, "*Raven*." They signalled back, "OK."

Slowly the *Butatres* came above the wind on our windward side. They shot a line to us with their line launcher. It became hung up in the triatic stay, and we couldn't retrieve it. The line broke. Another shot, *bang, zzzt*, it missed. *Bang*, another line, again in the triatic. It

This photo accompanied the article "The Miracle of the Raven" by Cees van Staal. Translated from Dutch, the headline reads: "In the middle of a hurricane on a sinking yacht, TV actress Jean Aubrey and Captain Stengs saw a Ghost Ship."

broke again. *Bang, zzzt, zzzt*, a line once again into the shrouds; it broke again.

What was to happen now? *Butatres* came alongside But that wouldn't be possible, I thought. In these seas? When she came within ten metres, a heaving line fell on our decks, followed by the towing cable. We grabbed it, we pulled on it, and we sweated, pulling on it well beyond our normal capacity. I wound it along the bowsprit and belayed it onto the large Samson post, once, twice, three times. And then the unbelievable happened. A big sea ran under us, the *Butatres* went down in a deep trough and our bowsprit hooked onto her companion-

The sinking *Raven* is towed into Musel, Spain.

way, tore it off, and swayed away with it. Another big wave, we swayed toward the *Butatres* again, she went down again, so did we, and then, as we swayed toward her again, the companionway was placed back on her railing, where it belonged, while our bowsprit swayed out from underneath it. We were free!

I looked at Captain Francisco Grande Alvarez and bowed to him. He grinned.

At eight o'clock in the morning of January 22, the *Raven* was passed on to the tug *Torres* near the shores of Musel. We were freezing cold. Inside the ship, the water was up to deck level. Only at the bow and the stern was there some space between the water level and decks. The *Torres* pumped 200 tons of water out of our 282 cubic metres of interior volume: 20 tons more than our 180 tons of weight-carrying capacity. In theory, this would be impossible

176

without sinking or capsizing. But, as I said at the beginning of my story, that was the miracle of the *Raven*.

After the Miracle

Raven's survival made many naval architects curious. Several came to examine her while she was in the Spanish shipyard. They took measurements and did calculations and came to the conclusion that *Raven* did not sink because she was a wooden ship, and this, together with her sheer, which allowed her to maintain some buoyancy in her forward and stern quarters, was the reason she remained afloat. She definitely should have capsized. But she didn't. So that remained a big question, and a logical explanation for her remaining upright was never found. *Raven*'s upright position, and the lack of change in her rolling period when she was virtually full of water, remained mysteries.

Another letter concerning the *Raven*, from Denmark, told us a bit more about the ship's history. When she was built and had come off the ways of the shipyard, she was taken to the quay to be tied alongside. The owner, the man for whom the ship had been built, was on board at the time. As the ship came close to the quay, he jumped off to take a mooring line ashore but missed the quay and fell between the ship and the quay. He was crushed to death. This was the man, according to several other reports, who had been seen on board; the one who opened doors, turned lights off and on, and who, according to her description, Joan Whiteley saw shortly before we hit the reef.

The *Raven* had clearly been a mystery ship for a long time. Now she lay at rest on a reef between Ile de la Gonâve and that finger of Haiti's main island that extends to the west. This should have been the end of the story, but it wasn't.

Chapter Twenty-One

We had been back in Vancouver for about a month when we received a message from the customs broker: the container that held the *Raven*'s salvaged goods had been diverted from Vancouver to Seattle. Bert, Ray, and I decided to rent a truck and drive down to Seattle to pick up the goods.

When we arrived at the port we were taken to the container, which now sat in an area where many other containers were stored. The port employee compared the identification numbers on the containers with those written on a piece of paper attached to a clipboard. "Here it is," he said, after double-checking the numbers and letters. "Yeah, that's the one." He took a key from a chain hanging around his neck and opened the lock that secured the rear doors of the container. "She's all yours," he said and went on his way.

We backed the truck close to the container doors and opened them. What we saw when we looked inside gave all three of us a start. The evil-faced pirate was staring at us. It lay on the floor, right in front of all the other boxes and articles stored in the container. After a moment's shocked silence, Ray was the first to react.

"That bloody thing again!" he yelled.

"But, but you threw it overboard, didn't you?" I stammered. "I saw you do it!" I was beginning to doubt myself. Had I gone crazy? "You did, didn't you? Throw it overboard, I mean?"

"Yes," said Ray. "Absolutely—no question about it."

"So how did it get in here?" Bert said.

My brain had started working again, in search of an answer. "It must have been the Haitian natives," I said. "They must have retrieved it and thrown it back on board."

"But then," Bert replied, "how did it get into this container? I don't remember anyone taking that thing off the *Raven* and putting it on the freighter. And I certainly don't recall taking it off the freighter and putting it into the truck. Do you?"

"Well," said Ray, "however it got here, I'm going to make sure it won't pester us again."

With an expression of repulsion on his face, he apprehensively picked up the statue. He held the pirate's head above the pavement, then smashed it onto the concrete. Determined to finish the job, he ground the pieces into dust by stepping on them with the heels of his shoes, twisting his toes from side to side. All that remained was a chalky powder that would soon be washed away by the rain.

During our drive back to Vancouver, we didn't speak of the

subject again. But although we were avoiding it, it certainly remained in the forefront of our minds.

Even with the statue gone, our misadventure had not ended.

Earlier, I had purchased insurance for the *Raven*. Joan had delivered the preliminary papers to me when she arrived in Nassau. The policy had not yet been issued: only a cover note existed, stating that the vessel was insured. A cover note had also been issued for a separate liability policy to cover us in case of passenger injury. When I returned to Vancouver, I submitted a claim to the insurance company; the *Raven* was in fact insured by a number of companies, which had each underwritten a portion of the insured amount.

Not long after submitting the claim, I was informed of lawsuits against me from some of the individuals who had left the boat in Haiti. Instead of boarding a flight home, the four musketeers had booked passage on a cruise ship and were demanding that I should pay for their cruise. Jack Owens stated that he had broken his leg as a result of the shipwreck, and he wanted to be compensated for that.

I had no choice but to hire a lawyer. The first one I hired was referred to me by an acquaintance. This turned out to be a big mistake. I didn't realize that the lawyer specialized in divorces. Not only did he not know how to handle my case (he filed the wrong papers), but he also lost some of the documents I had given to him, including the cover note for the liability insurance that was needed to protect me from the suing crew. As a result, that company denied it had provided coverage. Without the cover note, I couldn't prove otherwise.

Having fired the first lawyer, I hired a new one, and this one knew his stuff. First, he arranged an interview with Jack Owens to inform him that the entire crew would be able to testify that Jack had broken his leg in Great Inagua several days before the *Raven* hit the reef, so how could he have broken his leg as a result of the shipwreck? Then he asked Jack if his wife would be present in the courtroom while he was being questioned about having been seen with his broken leg in Haiti, also prior to the shipwreck, while enjoying the company of another woman. Jack Owens dropped the case.

The four musketeers never made it to the courtroom either. After my lawyer questioned them, they too changed their minds. That was a big relief.

Now, however, the companies insuring the *Raven* denied the claim because we hadn't gone to Miami but had started the cruise in Nassau instead. Had the boat come to Miami, they told us, they would have arranged for a survey there. Yet they had accepted Ron Turner's survey, which had been submitted to them; and they had never told me that a survey was to be done in Miami.

Fighting with insurance companies is like fighting any giant corporation. They know all the tricks and have all the money to carry them out. Their main tactics were delaying actions: postpone, postpone, postpone.

Our battle lasted more than five years, steadily draining my resources, which had already been depleted by the bills I had to pay as a result of the shipwreck: the flights of the crew, refunds, hotel accommodation, and so on. We had already put a second mortgage on our house to pay those expenses.

I had come to the bottom of the pit. We went back to work

with our sailing school but were barely able to survive because of the seemingly endless expenses.

About a month after the shipwreck, when I was still expecting to recover by collecting from the insurance companies, I started searching for another vessel. On a trip to the Caribbean for this purpose, I was accompanied by Glen Kinnee, a friend who was to become my business partner. On our way back to Vancouver, we were routed via Haiti, where we would catch an Air France flight. As we waited to board the aircraft, I spotted the pilot who was to fly us home and asked him what route he would be taking. Noticing his puzzled look, I explained that I would be interested in taking a picture of the wreck of the *Raven* and told him of its location. He replied that he would keep it in mind, and he asked me what my seat number was.

Shortly after takeoff, the stewardess approached me and said that the captain wanted to see me. She guided me through a door into the flight cabin. The pilot and a co-pilot were seated behind the controls. Another person, probably the flight engineer, was seated off to one side, monitoring what I thought to be engine instruments and radio equipment. I was told to take a seat behind the pilot, and a set of earphones was put on my head. Through the headset I heard the control tower speaking to the pilots, something about raising the altitude to twelve thousand feet.

"Roger," said the pilot. "Twelve thousand feet."

At this time the plane was still flying low, perhaps a couple of hundred feet above ground, and I could see no indication that the pilot was making any effort to rise above that level. He turned around and took his headphones off, indicating that I should do the same.

"You have to tell us where the wreck is. We're flying in the direction you indicated, but I don't know exactly where it would be."

I stretched and looked out through the windshield. "A little bit to port," I said. "It's about twelve miles south of Ile de la Gonâve. There! Yes, there it is."

I grabbed my camera, but it was too late—we had already passed it.

"Let's take another look," the pilot said. He grabbed the controls, and the plane started to turn.

On our second pass I had a better look and managed to shoot a photo through one of the side windows. There wasn't much left of the *Raven*: just the outline of the hull, all of it under water.

"How was that?" said the pilot.

"That was great," I answered. "Thank you very much." I stood up, said goodbye to the other two crew members, and returned to my seat.

As I walked back through the cabin, I noticed the other passengers looking at me with suspicion. I had the feeling that something strange was going on. As it turned out, I was correct.

When I sat down next to Glen, he said, "You had the passengers in a bit of a panic. First they saw you following the stewardess to the flight cabin. Then the plane started to turn. They thought you had forced the stewardess to take you to the pilot's cabin and then hijacked the plane."

"Oh my God!" I said. I looked around at the other passengers, who were still observing me closely. "That never occurred to me." I tried to appear nonchalant. Perhaps that would calm their fears.

The plane started to climb and settled on a steady course. Soon the passengers relaxed.

I doubt that a pilot from any other airline would have been so co-operative in helping me find the remains of the *Raven*.

About a month later I found a boat that I thought could be a substitute for the *Raven*. I bought her with the help of a bank loan guaranteed by Glen Kinnee. This boat, a 114-foot, ketch-rigged, luxury charter yacht called *Ring Andersen*, was already booked with charters and based in Grenada. The boat was fully staffed with a captain and crew. Part of the agreement of sale was that Glen and I would honour the charters that had been booked. After that, I would move her to Vancouver, where we could use her in the program with the kids.

However, shortly after the purchase, the captain became seriously ill and had to return to England, his home country. Bert had already started another job and was not available, so I had to take over the ship and carry out the charters. After a few months on the *Ring Andersen*, enjoying the lifestyle on this beautiful vessel, I decided to abandon our struggles with the underprivileged children program and remain in the Caribbean permanently. We rented out our house, and Elise and our two daughters joined me in Grenada. This move also necessitated the sale of the Vancouver Academy of Sailing

Every time something came up in regard to the court proceedings, I had to fly from the Caribbean back to Vancouver. I also had to fly Ron Turner, who had done the survey of the *Raven*, from Nassau to Vancouver to testify as a witness, adding to the expenses. But we were doing well in the charter business.

Finally the court reached a decision: the insurance companies had to pay. This sounds exciting, but there was no victory yet; the insurance companies appealed the case. When eventually the appeals were completed, most of the companies on the policy were no longer in business. The portion of the coverage provided by the remaining insurance company was so small that it wasn't enough to pay for the expenses of the proceedings.

Another loss was Danny Tanaka's film footage, which had been introduced into the court's records to give the judge some idea of *Raven*'s condition both before and after she hit the reef. Danny had remained on board until he was taken off the ship by the Haitian navy, faithfully recording everything that had occurred. When we tried to retrieve the film footage, we were told that it had been misplaced. After several attempts to locate it, we resigned ourselves to accepting that it had been lost forever.

Chapter Twenty-Two

A lot of events occurred after the *Raven* misery—some bad, some good. About a year after we had settled in the Caribbean, Elise and I parted company. A few years later, both of us remarried. I met my new wife, Jules, in the Caribbean, and together, assisted by six crew, we operated the *Ring Andersen* in the charter business. We were successful, and I was able to climb out of the financial hole created by the sinking of the *Raven*. We bought Glen's share of the company and became the sole owners of our charter operation.

In 1980, Jules and I sold the *Ring Andersen* and returned to Canada where, in addition to my work as a marine surveyor, I told the stories of our adventures in the Caribbean in the book *No Shoes Allowed* and its sequel, *Gone to Come Back*.[1]

In 1995, some twenty-three years after the sinking of the

Raven, we bought a house in Langley, British Columbia. Our new home was constructed of big logs and had a cozy log-house interior, well suited to be decorated with some of the items I had taken from the *Raven*, which had been stowed in boxes and moved several times to various locations over the years.

I was sitting on the floor of the living room in front of the fireplace. Tables, chairs, and boxes of goods were all around me—the furniture waiting to be put into place, the boxes waiting to be unpacked. Gathered by the kitchen door were items from the *Raven*—brass lamps, the ship's name board, and the decorative guns. The swords had somehow disappeared in Port-au-Prince.

As I was unpacking one of the boxes, Jules was behind me, unwrapping things. Suddenly, I had the feeling that something was wrong. I looked behind me and saw Jules standing up straight, staring at the kitchen door with a strange expression on her face.

"What's the matter?" I asked. "What are you looking at?" I glanced at the kitchen door but saw nothing unusual.

"There ... there's a man standing there," she said, pointing at the kitchen door. "He's looking at those *Raven* things."

"What are you talking about?" I said. "There's no one there."

"Yes there is. Look, don't you see him? He's looking at all that *Raven* stuff. But," she said, "I can see through him, I can see that light switch behind him. He can't be real ... it's a ghost!"

Please, not again, I thought.

"What does he look like?" I asked. "Describe him to me."

"He's wearing a cap, a fisherman's cap. And a blue jacket, and blue, old-fashioned trousers. The type that old fishermen wear in Holland—you know, those trousers that go with the traditional costume. Oh! Now he's gone. He's suddenly disappeared!" Jules's face had turned white.

I was convinced that she was not making this up; she was serious and was convinced that she had seen the apparition. Jules had of course heard the *Raven* story, but she had never heard such a detailed description of the ghost. The result of this sighting was that my treasures from the *Raven* were once more put away in boxes and stored in the garage. There was no way I could persuade Jules to allow them into the house.

Thinking about ghosts and the *Raven* makes me wonder about paranormal events and experiences. There must be some truth in them. My experience with the *Raven* certainly suggests that there is.

It has also made me think about another unexplained incident. This one occurred after the sinking of the *Raven*, when we were sailing the *Ring Andersen* from Grenada to St. Thomas in the Virgin Islands. Again it was at night. I was off watch. I had gone to my bunk and was sound asleep when suddenly I woke up with a bad feeling in my stomach. Something was amiss, but I didn't know what it was. I went on deck to the steering station and checked the chart and the last position that had been plotted.

"Are you certain this is where we are?" I asked the man on watch.

"Yes, I just checked our position," he answered.

"Let's check it again," I said.

"Why?"

"I don't know. I just have an uneasy feeling."

We checked the position again and, sure enough, the

previous position was incorrect. If we had stayed on that course, we would have ended up on Saba Bank, an area of shallow water with sandbanks and reefs dead ahead of us. We quickly made a course change to prevent a grounding. Somehow, someone or something had warned me. Unfortunately that had not been the case during the *Raven* escapade.

This type of intuitive knowing is not uncommon. There have been other instances when I was at sea that a feeling of something amiss crept into me, and every time there was a good reason for that feeling. I have heard of similar experiences from other sailors.

Joshua Slocum, in his book *Sailing Alone Around the World*, describes an interesting experience he had. While sailing somewhere in the Atlantic Ocean, he became sick from food poisoning and was incapable of tending to his vessel for several days. One day he looked up from his bunk and saw a man standing in the cockpit. The man was sailing and steering his boat. When Slocum confronted him, the man introduced himself: "I am one of Columbus's crew . . . I am the pilot of the *Pinta* come to aid you. Lie quiet, Señor captain . . . and I will guide your ship tonight."[1] The man mysteriously disappeared when Slocum's condition improved, allowing him once again to operate the vessel himself. According to Slocum, the pilot of the *Pinta* had been in control for several days, making sail changes and keeping the boat on its proper course.

To this day, I have been unable to find a logical explanation for the many strange things that happened on the *Raven* and the related misfortunes that seemed to drag on for such a

1. Joshua Slocum, *Sailing Alone Around the World* (1900; rep. Köln: Könemann, 1997), 38.

long time afterward. Ron Turner, whom I found to be a pretty sober and logical man, surprised me when he was in Vancouver to testify as a witness, when he said, "The ghost of the *Raven* wanted that ship to go down so desperately that nothing could have stopped it. It's too bad that you happened to be the owner when he finally succeeded." Ron was the last man from whom I would have expected that type of remark.

In rethinking the whole situation, I still wonder if his observation was correct. If there was a ghost and he was the original owner of the ship, was he angry because the name of his ship had been changed from *Danebrog* to *Raven*? Is that why he wanted to sink the *Raven*? Or had he tried to save her? After all, the boat did not sink during the storm in the Bay of Biscay. For some mysterious reason, which naval architects could not determine, the *Raven* stayed upright in defiance of gravity. Then there was the ghost's appearance in Joan's cabin. Had he perhaps tried to warn us that we were heading for a reef? The question remains: did he want to sink the ship, or had he tried to save her?

I hope that my telling the story of the *Raven* receives the ghost's blessing and puts his tortured soul to rest.

As I was writing this account of the *Raven*'s last voyage, I made
a startling discovery that may connect the *Raven*, through an
interesting twist of fate, to the *Mary Celeste*, the ship that has
puzzled people for many years. In the *Mary Celeste*'s case, the
puzzle concerns the mysterious disappearance of the ship's crew
before she was found sailing, crewless, off the Azores in the
1800s. After some of the salvage crew sailed her to Gibraltar,
the *Mary Celeste* changed owners several times. Her last owner
reportedly wrecked the ship on purpose in the Caribbean in
1884 or 1885 to claim the insurance money.

What caught my attention was an article by the National
Underwater and Marine Agency (NUMA), which I found on
the Internet.[1] It reported that Clive Cussler, the well-known
author and discoverer of shipwrecks, had found the wreck of

1. National Underwater and Marine Agency, "Legendary Ghost Ship, Mary Celeste,
Discovered on a Reef in Haiti," press release, August 8, 2001, http://www.numa.net/
press/080801.html.

the *Mary Celeste* in 2001. Of particular interest to me was the location of Cussler's discovery: a reef near Haiti!

Could this be the same reef on which the *Raven* had been wrecked?

The NUMA report stated clearly that the discoverers and scientists, after carrying out detailed research and a survey of the reef, found no evidence of another wreck on that reef. It also stated that samples and artifacts retrieved from the wreckage were proved to be from the *Mary Celeste*.

The artifacts, as far as I could determine from the report, consisted of pieces of wood, a fastening, and a piece of Muntz metal, a sheathing of 60 percent copper alloy that was used for plating on the bottoms of boats to repel marine growth and deter shipworms. The dimensions of the remains of the vessel—approximately one hundred feet long and twenty-five feet wide—were consistent with the size of the *Mary Celeste*. Those measurements were also similar to the *Raven*'s length and width.

As I continued reading the report, my interest grew. The description of the now-charted reef, Rochelois Reef, mentioned a small islet nearby, populated by about 120 natives. That sounded familiar to me, and I couldn't help remembering the natives we met when the *Raven* grounded. I compared the coordinates of our grounding with the coordinates of Rochelois Reef. They were exactly the same.[1]

1. As I mentioned earlier, the older chart we had on the *Raven* did not show this reef, but, until recently, Caribbean charts were badly outdated; many places in that region hadn't been surveyed since the late 1800s. I remember sailing in 1972 from Grenada to Tobago with a chart that was terribly inaccurate. Since we were commissioned to do a few cruises along the coast of Tobago, we ended up spending several days carefully exploring the area to update the chart we had, taking bearings on coastal structures and other visibly identifiable features. Sailors who frequented the Caribbean in the

If the survey carried out by the discoverers of the *Mary Celeste* indicated that there was evidence of only one shipwreck on that reef, it had to be the *Raven*, not the *Mary Celeste*, didn't it? Or could it be both?

I started corresponding with Scott St. George, one of the scientists who had examined the recovered artifacts. To my surprise, St. George said that the wood samples he had examined were longleaf pine. This species of tree is native to the southeastern United States and is found along the coastal plain from eastern Texas to southeast Virginia, extending into northern and central Florida. According to St. George, the samples of longleaf pine he had examined could not have come from the *Mary Celeste* because they were from trees that were still growing when the *Mary Celeste* was built. (Apparently scientists can determine both the age of a tree and the time when that tree was growing.) He also said that his findings should have been included in NUMA's final report, but I could find no trace of them.

In addition to St. George's opinion about the age of the wood, I thought it was unlikely that the *Mary Celeste*, which was built in Nova Scotia, would have been constructed of longleaf pine. As far as I knew, ships built in Nova Scotia, such as the *Bluenose*, were built with local timber. Exotic woods imported from distant areas would not have been used for building working vessels, certainly not in the nineteenth century.

The *Raven* was built of oak and beech wood, but we had used longleaf pine for the modifications we did in Nassau. It was possible that not much of the original oak and beech

1970s and 1980s were well aware of the inaccuracy of the charts and would use charts and cruising information published by local sailors, such as Chris Doyle and Don Street. The use of satellites and GPS have allowed chart makers to considerably refine the accuracy of charts, especially in this region.

remained in the wreck; those types of wood deteriorate rapidly when exposed to moisture, especially in a warm climate. Longleaf pine, on the other hand, has been a valuable source for naval stores—for resin, turpentine, and timber for ships. It is saturated with resin and is known for its ability to resist rot. Could the wood samples found on the reef have belonged to the *Raven* instead of the *Mary Celeste*?

Another thing I found strange was the fastening. The NUMA report stated that it was a typical fastening used only in the days when the *Mary Celeste* was built, but when I studied a picture of the object in a film clip about the discovery that I saw on the History Channel, I thought it looked like a typical boat spike that is still used in the building of large wooden ships. I must admit, however, that I only saw a picture of that nail; there may have been other facts relating to this object that indicated it was unique to shipbuilding in the mid-1800s.

The Muntz metal found with the wreck apparently replaced copper sheathing in the latter 1800s. The *Raven* was sheathed with what we called copper sheathing, but most likely it was actually Muntz metal. In any event, that sheathing was fastened to a large section of the bottom to act as a ground plate for the single-sideband radio and to protect against an invasion of sea worms, those nasty creatures that eat into wooden planking, causing significant damage and weakening the boat's structure. Many Baltic traders had, and many still have, this type of plating on their bottoms. Also, the entire bottom of the *Ring Andersen*, the boat we operated in the Caribbean, was plated with this material.

The discovery of the *Mary Celeste* occurred in 2001, almost thirty years after the *Raven* foundered on that reef. The records state that the *Mary Celeste* sank around 1885, about eighty-seven years before the *Raven* sank. Apparently the wreck Clive Cussler found was completely overgrown with coral. One might think that this much coral would not have covered the *Raven*, since she had been on the reef for less than thirty years. However, having lived in the Caribbean and having been involved with ships and yachts almost all my life, I knew that coral grew in that region at an alarming rate. Boats in cooler climates need to have their bottoms cleaned about once every two years, and even if left for three years, they show relatively little marine growth—usually barnacles and mussels, and perhaps some seaweed, depending on where they are located. In the Caribbean, if a boat is left tied to a dock, you must clean its bottom almost every six months.

I once left the *Ring Andersen* in the water without cleaning her bottom for a whole year. When we hauled her out, the growth was well over four inches thick—not just barnacles, but all kinds of encrustation of marine growth—even though we had been sailing her regularly. The bottom looked like a coral reef! Extend that to thirty years, and it would have built up to more than ten feet, about three metres. To back this up, the Geoscience Research Institute has reported that in some cases coral will grow 414 millimetres (more than 16 inches) per year. In the case of the *Ring Andersen*, the growth had accumulated over the bottom, the area that was coated with copper sheathing (Muntz metal?) and a good layer of antifouling paint. In the case of the *Raven*, lying broken up on the reef, the inside of the wreck was exposed. That area was not coated with anti-fouling paint or Muntz sheathing. The growth of marine life would therefore have been much greater.

Another thing that puzzled me was a statement in the report from Allan Gardner, the skipper of the NUMA survey boat. He said that the *Mary Celeste* created a large trench, or groove, to or from the islet when she rammed the coral, and that this groove was now used as a channel by the natives to launch their boats from their island. This didn't make sense to me. The wreck was found on a reef some distance away from where the natives were living. If the ship made a groove in the coral, it would eventually come to rest at the end of the groove. In other words, since the wreck was found on a reef some distance from the natives' residence, and since the groove led from the island to the offshore wreck, the ship would have had to ram into the natives' little island first and than run across it in order to finally come to a halt in the location where it was found. If this was what happened, which I find hard to believe, there would also be a trench or groove across the natives' islet. Obviously, the ship came from a different direction, going past or toward the islet, and could not have left a trench that went to the little habitat. Furthermore, the ship could not have made much of a trench anyway, since it would have come to a stop almost immediately after grounding, as the *Raven* did. The *Mary Celeste* was thought to have been sailing in an easterly direction—in other words, into the prevailing wind; if that were the case, she would not have left a trench. Even if, for some reason, the usual wind direction had changed and she'd had the wind behind her, as we did on the *Raven*, the length of trench would have been minuscule.

The origin of the trench may be tied up with another thing that puzzled me: why wasn't the *Raven*'s engine found when NUMA discovered the wreck? If it was still on the reef, even

if it was buried well beneath the coral, the scientists, with the aid of their sonar equipment, should have located it. There was no mention of it in the report. But perhaps that engine was no longer on the reef. It's possible that the natives dismantled it and took it away in parts. After all, they had been effective in removing virtually everything else that was salvageable—my flight over the wreck shortly after the grounding demonstrated the natives' eager activity in disassembling the *Raven*. The masts, rigging, and deck structure had already been removed; only the bare hull was still visible. But they had no boats capable of carrying the massive engine, even if they removed some of its components. Perhaps they dragged the large engine through the coral to the island, *thereby making the trench*. With the aid of cables, ropes, and enough manpower, this would certainly have been a possibility.

Besides the trench, there was a new structure on the islet: when I watched the video I saw a raised structure on four metal posts, a sort of tower, probably supporting a light to serve as a beacon. That structure wasn't there in 1972, and this story would have turned out very differently if it had been.

Since the archaeologists stated without any doubt that they had found the *Mary Celeste*, it seemed likely to me that mixed in with the artifacts found on the reef were some that belonged to the *Raven*. I tried to contact the various individuals and organizations involved in the discovery, but except for the prompt response from Scott St. George and some of the maritime museums I contacted, I received no reply and thought I had reached a dead end.

However, about a month after my inquiry, I received a phone call from Dr. James Delgado, the archaeologist who

determined that the artifacts retrieved from the wreck were indeed from the *Mary Celeste*. He apologized for the delay in responding and said that he had been out of the country. When I asked him about the longleaf pine, he said they had also found oak in the wreck and determined that it had come from the *Mary Celeste*. When I asked him about the evidence of only one wreck on the site, he replied that there was in fact some evidence of another wreck. An anchor had been found some distance from the wreck. I wondered if that was the anchor we had used to try to pull the *Raven* off the reef. We talked about the amount of coral covering the wreck, and he said that yes, in the Caribbean region, that amount of coral could have accumulated in only thirty years.

I had more questions for Dr. Delgado, but he explained that since he did not have the appropriate file at hand, he unfortunately would not be able to provide me with any further details or answers. I hoped he would call me again when he had the file, but he never did.

Although my conversation with Dr. Delgado cleared up some of my puzzles, the discovery of the *Mary Celeste* has raised more questions for me. Could it be that the *Raven* came to rest on top of the *Mary Celeste*? Could it be that the ghost of the *Raven* is playing tricks again and wants to fool us into believing that the *Raven* and the *Mary Celeste* are one and the same? What happened to the crew of the *Mary Celeste*? Perhaps *Raven*'s ghost knows the answer.

Jan de Groot was born in Holland and has been involved with boats and ships since early childhood. After serving several years in the merchant marine, he spent close to ten years in the Caribbean in the yacht-charter trade. He is now a marine surveyor and resides in Langley, British Columbia, Canada.

Other books by Jan de Groot include *Buying the Right Boat*, a how-to book for potential boat buyers (1994); *No Shoes Allowed* (1996) and its sequel *Gone to Come Back* (2000), about the adventures of a sailor in the Caribbean charter trade; and *A Boy in War*, a memoir of the occupation of war-torn Holland during the Second World War (Sono Nis Press, 2008).

Yachties in Paradise, a combined and revised edition of *No Shoes Allowed* and *Gone to Come Back*, will soon be published by Sono Nis Press.